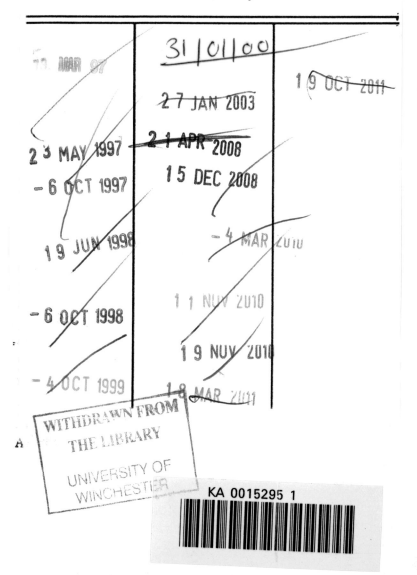

# Partnership for Change:
# Parents and Schools

Other books by Ronald G. Cave

STAYING ON

With D. A. F. Conochie
LIVING WITH OTHER PEOPLE

With Raymond O'Malley
THINKING AND TALKING

LIVING WITH THE MASS MEDIA

EDUCATION FOR PERSONAL
RESPONSIBILITY

Published by Penguin Books
ALL THEIR FUTURE

# Partnership for Change: Parents and Schools

## Ronald G. Cave

Senior County Inspector of Schools
Cambridgeshire and the Isle of Ely

## Ward Lock Educational

ISBN 0 7062 3302 6
First published 1970

Set in 11 on 13 point Monophoto Baskerville
Made in England
Printed by Cox & Wyman Ltd., London, Fakenham and Reading
for Ward Lock Educational Company Limited 116 Baker Street London W1M 2BB

# Contents

# Acknowledgments

I am most grateful to the authors and publishers who have so freely given permission for the reproduction of copyright material. My debt is also great to the many friends and colleagues who have generously allowed me to make use of their notes and reports. Where opinions are expressed these are of course entirely my own and do not necessarily coincide with the views of my employer, the Cambridgeshire and Isle of Ely Education Committee.

Our argument in this and the following chapters is that educational policy should explicitly recognize the power of the environment upon the school and of the school upon the environment. Teachers are linked to parents by the children for whom they are both responsible. The triangle should be completed and a more direct relationship established between teachers and parents. They should be partners in more than name; their responsibility become joint instead of several.

*Children and Their Primary Schools*
HMSO

# FROM SCHOOL BOARD
# TO SEEBOHM

Although teachers in training spend a great deal of valuable time studying the history of education, few appear to remember very much about this subject once they enter the schools and more practical matters engage their attention. It is not surprising therefore that it is comparatively rare to meet anyone outside the profession who has any detailed knowledge of the historical background to our present system, and occasionally one meets with confused notions in the most unexpected quarters. For example I have been introduced to a parent teacher association meeting as 'Mr Cave, the School Inspector,' followed by the additional, but erroneous, piece of information: 'Better known in our own young days as the School Board Man.' (The chairman who made this odd introduction was a doctor who could hardly have been older than his late thirties.) The story that one of our post-war prime ministers expressed genuine surprise on hearing that fees were not charged in secondary modern schools may be apocryphal—but the tale somehow has a ring of truth about it.

Such instances are probably not typical but it might be useful to begin this book, which it is hoped will be read by parents as well as teachers, with a brief description of the growth of compulsory education in this country, against which recent developments, especially the trend towards improved home/school cooperation, may be judged.

Long before the state accepted any financial responsibility for education, there were a large number of schools in existence, some of them of ancient origin. At the beginning of the nineteenth century, in addition to the misleadingly named public schools, there were company schools, guild schools, parish schools, dame schools—in fact schools of almost infinite variety and quality. Of the voluntary schools for the poor, only a very few were self-supporting on the fees paid by parents; for the most part such schools were dependent on charity of one form or another. The largest group of voluntary schools were the church elementary schools, usually founded and maintained by the local clergy. (It is of interest to note that the Catholic Church was forbidden by law to open voluntary schools until 1829.) Even with all this charitable provision, in the first half of the nineteenth century large numbers of poor children received no education at all. A survey made in Manchester in the 1830s showed that 'Out of every 10 children of school age, 4 went to no school at all, 3 went to Sunday Schools only, 2 attended the very unsatisfactory dame and common day schools, and only 1 received any education that was considered satisfactory to the investigating committee.'[1]

Inevitably, under such a laissez-faire system, the standard of elementary education varied considerably. It is hardly surprising that so many of the common day schools were unsatisfactory when one considers the fact that the pay, even of a competent schoolmaster, might be no more than £20 or £30 a year without board. Many were far from competent. Two schoolmasters, no doubt concerned about the standing of their profession in the eyes of the general public, wrote to one of the educational papers in 1851 saying: 'Till within these few years, any poor, lame, deaf, decrepit or broken fortuned man who was likely to require a share of the poor rate was considered fit for the office of schoolmaster.'[2] One can only wonder about the educational standards reached by the pupils of a certain Roger Giles of Devonshire, who advertised himself as 'Surgin, Parish clark and Skulemaster, Groser and Undertaker. (ps—I tayches gografy, rithmetic, cowsticks, jimnastics and other chynees tricks.')[3]

Less than 100 years ago there were a great many influential

people who saw little profit in educating the children of the poor, except in such useful skills as needlework and netting. It is disheartening to note that many of the current arguments against raising the school leaving age and expanding higher education are couched in almost identical terms to the ones used to attack the establishment of compulsory education in the ninteeenth century. Then, as is so often the case now, people whose own full-time education had often been continued into the late teens or early twenties saw little sense in educating 'young toughs'. Much is written at present, in both the popular and educational press, about the difficulties of educating and disciplining reluctant pupils, especially in the educational priority areas. How much greater were the problems of the early educational reformers, who faced large classes of young but really tough pupils, many of them unwashed, unshod, verminous and as truculent as their state of malnutrition would allow them to be. To the opponents of universal education it seemed self-evident that the young of the poor would be far better off in the fields or the factory. Even in that commercially conscious age, when some economists were already postulating a positive relationship between economic growth and universal education, there were many who saw the dangers of compulsory schooling as more real than any possible advantages.

Two voluntary societies were in the foreground of educational advance—the National Society, which acted for the Church of England, and the British and Foreign Schools Society, founded by Quakers and incorporating the Royal Lancasterian Society. At that stage in our social history, education for the children of the poor remained very much a missionary activity. From time to time efforts were made to bring the voluntary schools into a unified system; these failed mainly because of religious rather than educational difficulties.

In 1833 the government began the practice of making a small annual grant to the voluntary societies. An unsuccessful attempt had been made to obtain public money for elementary education in 1807, and a proposal made in 1820 that treasury assistance should be given to the building of schools also failed. The amount of the first grant to the societies was £20,000. (As a comparison it has been estimated that in 1969 public expenditure on education was in the region of two thousand million pounds.) It was a stipulation of the first grant that for every pound of public money spent another had to be raised by voluntary subscription. A condition somewhat reminiscent of the system exists in some areas today: expensive or unusual items of equipment are sometimes purchased on a pound for pound basis by a grant from the local authority, matched by a similar sum from school funds. We may gain some appreciation of the amount of voluntary effort in the early days by noting that out of fifteen-and-a-half million pounds spent on school building between 1839 and 1876, less than two million was contributed by the exchequer. As there was no existing administrative machinery through which the early grants could be channelled, the money was entrusted, following recommendation by one of the two great voluntary societies, to those individual citizens who had made themselves responsible for setting up and maintaining schools.

Although Kay Shuttleworth, when he was appointed Secretary of the Committee of Council for Education in 1839, sought to establish the principle of school management as a matter for lay participation, in practice it was usually the local clergy who had the most to do with the everyday administration of the schools. The Cross Commission, reporting in 1888, emphasized again the need for a group of responsible individuals associated with each school, but under the 1902 Act, apart from voluntary schools, managing bodies were required only for schools provided by county councils. County boroughs and the smaller authorities were permitted either to have or not to have managing bodies, as they thought fit. It was up to the local education authorities to determine the powers of the managing body; in some areas these were trivial, but in London managers were charged with drawing up an annual report, checking school records, inspecting premises and equipment, advising on the appointment of staff, investigating complaints against teachers, promoting visits of educational value and helping in arrangements for school meals, play centres, school savings banks and school open days.[4] It was not until the 1944 Education Act that all the schools which were maintained by local authorities were required to have a body of managers.

During the debate on the 1944 Act it was moved that managing bodies should include at least one manager to be representative of the parents. This motion attracted considerable support and little opposition, although reference was made to the possible difficulties of recruiting parents where a school had no parent teacher association. Mr Chuter Ede, speaking for the government, expressed sympathy with the motion but thought there would be difficulty in the selection of representatives and suggested that it should be left to the managers to see that at least one of their members represented the parents. He hoped that local education authorities would note the discussion, and the amendment was then withdrawn. This obviously sound proposal did not meet the voluntary acceptance hoped for by Mr Chuter Ede; years later the Plowden Committee[5] had yet again to recommend that parents should be recruited as managers. It seems probable that the new Education Act, promised by the Labour Government, will make it compulsory that parents should be represented on boards of governors and managing bodies, but it is indicative of the often slow pace of educational change that so obvious a reform has been for so long delayed.

To return to our historical survey. In the 1860s the principle of payment by results was introduced. Announcing this innovation, the vice president of the new Education Department, Mr Robert Lowe, said 'I cannot promise the House that this system will be an economical one and I cannot promise that it will be an efficient one, but I can promise that it shall be either one or the other.' Under this system the size of the government grant was determined by average attendance and the pupils' performance in an examination. To ensure the largest possible grant, children were sometimes carried from their sick beds to sit the examination and many stories are told of ingenious methods, devised by teachers and connived at by both parents and pupils, to beat the examiner. This system, although in a modified form after 1882, remained in force until the 1902 Act set up an entirely new structure for public education and made the schools the responsibility of local education authorities. The school boards, which were established under the 1870 Act, had the power to make bylaws and enforce school attendance for children between the ages of five and thirteen and, as we noted at the beginning of this chapter, the term 'school board man' is taking a long time to die in some areas. This is especially true of the northern industrial towns, where children unwilling to go to school may still be threatened by their parents: 'The school board man will come for you.' It is hardly necessary to emphasize that today's education welfare officers are far removed from their predecessors, both in their approach to truancy and in the many other duties their work now embraces. The school boards had power to levy a rate to supplement the funds they received from state grants, subscriptions and fees. Compulsory school attendance was not entirely new, as various Factory Acts had laid down children's working hours and, in certain industries, enforced schooling from 1833 onwards. In fact, by the time of the first Elementary Education Act, some 85,000 children were already receiving some form of compulsory part-time education.

By the end of the nineteenth century, education was both compulsory and free in all but a few voluntary schools. In 1891 fees were abolished in schools under the direction of the school boards, although some voluntary schools continued to charge fees until 1918, when it was agreed that all elementary education should be free. At this time, of course, the term 'elementary education' meant exactly what it said. During most of the nineteenth century secondary education was confined almost entirely to the children of the well-to-do. There were notable exceptions in areas which had endowed local grammar schools, although it has been estimated that in 1894 the odds against gaining a scholarship to a secondary school were 270 to 1. Some of the 'most intelligent and moral pupils' who attended the elementary schools gained a Queen's Scholarship and went on to training college. As we have noted, the 1902 Act made the schools the responsibility of local education authorities, who had the duty of maintaining and keeping efficient all public elementary schools, whether voluntary or board. In addition they had the power to provide secondary and higher education and from this date there was a steady growth in secondary education, although Huxley's 'ladder of learning' was at first much more like a slippery pole. The Education Act of 1918 laid a duty on the local education authorities to provide courses for the more able pupils and required all children to continue at school until the end of the term following their fourteenth birthday. In 1936 another Education Act recommended that the school leaving age should be raised to 15 as from 1st September 1939. The outbreak of the Second World War prevented this reform and it was not until 1947 that the leaving age was actually raised to 15. It was another 17 years before the Government announced that the leaving age would be raised to 16 in 1970/71. In January 1968 it was decided that the implementation of this decision would be deferred a further two years.

As the Second World War drew to a close the nation was forced to take stock of the end product of its educational system, and its conscience was stirred. The 1944 Act made education compulsory from the ages of 5 to 15 and provided for the raising of the school leaving age to 16 as soon as it was practicably possible. No longer was education enforced by bylaw but by the law of the land. Previously it had been the responsibility of the parents only to ensure that their child received 'efficient elementary instruction in reading, writing and arithmetic'. Now the law required that every child was to receive 'efficient full-time education suitable to his age, ability and aptitude either by regular attendance at school or otherwise'. Many parents do not realize that although the local authority must provide full facilities for education in the area for which it is responsible, if a suitable education can be provided in a child's home there is no compulsion to attend school. Some recent court cases however have shown how difficult it is for a parent to fully satisfy the 'age, ability and aptitude' requirement without considerable financial and advisory resources.

There is little point in a government legislating for universal compulsory education for its young, unless the same authority which enforces compulsion also takes a positive role in ensuring that the education which is provided is good. The past half century has seen the publication of a number of government-initiated reports, which have profoundly influenced not only the administration and organization of education but also the content of the curriculum and the way curriculum objectives are achieved in the actual classroom situation. Increasingly parents, and even the pupils themselves, are making significant contributions to the process of educational change and reform, although such bodies as the Advisory Centre for Education, the Home and School Council, the Association for the Advancement of State Education and the Comprehensive Schools' Committee are of recent growth, and the formation of federations of secondary school pupils, such as the Union of Secondary School Students, would have been unthinkable only a few years ago. The official government reports serve to acquaint the public as a whole with progressive developments and experiments and serve as a yardstick against which both parents and teachers can measure their own achievements and aspirations.

Between the years 1926 and 1933, a series of official reports, known after their chairman as the Hadow Reports, were of the utmost importance in shaping both the organization and content of our system of public education. In all there were three of these reports: *The Education of the Adolescent* (1926);[6] *The Primary School* (1931);[7] and *Infant and Nursery Schools* (1933).[8] Possibly the report which had the greatest immediate effect was *The Education of the Adolescent*, which enquired into 'the organization, objective and curriculum of courses of study suitable for children who will remain in full-time attendance at schools, other than secondary schools, up to the age of fifteen'. To a quite remarkable extent this report fixed the pattern of our system of education for many years to come, imposing a rigid and inflexible framework which even now is proving difficult to alter. The 1926 report, after making what today would be regarded as a physiologically and psychologically naïve statement that there is 'a tide which begins to rise in the veins of youth at the age of 11 or 12,' went on to advocate that there should be a break at the age of 11, after which secondary schooling should begin. It recommended that primary children in their fourth year should be set an examination which would decide whether they should go to a grammar school with an 'academic' bias or a modern school with a 'practical' approach. This suggestion set in motion the whole paraphernalia of the eleven-plus selection examination, an examination which has had as one of its side effects an increasing involvement on the part of the more concerned parent—a concern which became even more intense when fee paying at local authority grammar schools was abolished by the 1944 Act.

In the 1931 Report on *The Primary School*, it was advocated that the curriculum be thought of in terms of 'activity and experience, rather than knowledge to be acquired and facts to be stored'. Unfortunately, by the time of the publication of this report, the restrictive strait-jacket of attainment testing, with the consequent emphasis on preparation for selection, had already been fitted on the primary curriculum. The introduction of intelligence testing and other psychometric techniques did no more than add a little elastic to this strait-jacket. In the 1931 report, Sir Henry Hadow had written: 'What a wise and good parent will desire for his own children a nation must desire for all children,' thus echoing the words of the great American educationist, John Dewey, who had said 'What the best and wisest parent wants for his children that must the community want for all its children.' Having made this statement, the Hadow Report made no attempt to define the part that would be played by wise and good parents in the education of their children, and some of the difficulties of defining what is meant by a 'wise and good' parent will be discussed later in this book. Following on from the Hadow Reports, the Spens Report (1938)[9] recommended that there should be three distinct types of secondary schooling—grammar, technical and modern. Even at the time many teachers and parents felt that it would have made as much sense to sort the children into three groups on the basis of square heads, long heads and round heads!

Under the 1944 Act, two Central Advisory Councils were set up, one for England and one for Wales. It is of interest to note that it was necessary to stipulate that the councils should include 'persons who have had experience of the statutory system of public education as well as persons who have had experience of educational institutions not forming part of that system'. The first report of the Central Advisory Council dealt with the transition from school to independent life, the interests of children out of school and the problem of early leaving. Within a few years after the raising of the school leaving age to 15 in 1947, considerable concern was being expressed about the fact that many young people left school, as indeed they still do, at the earliest possible moment. This was not only true of secondary modern pupils but of young people who were following academic courses. The Central Advisory Council was asked to enquire into this problem and in 1954 issued their report *Early Leaving*,[10] which suggested that the influence of the home background was 'far reaching,' a pronouncement which is so obviously true in the light of our present knowledge that it has the appearance of an understatement. It was the first official report which recognized that few detailed research findings were available about the interaction of home and school, and the Council urged a prolonged and thorough investigation. In December 1959 the Council issued its report *Fifteen to Eighteen*,[11] which became known as the Crowther Report. Its terms of reference were 'to consider, in relation to the changing social and industrial needs of our society, and the needs of its individual citizens, the education of boys and girls between 15 and 18, and in particular to consider the balance at various levels of general and specialized studies between these ages and to examine the inter-relationship of the various stages of education'. Under the heading 'Education in a Changing World,' the Crowther Committee considered the growth in full-time education, the fact that most families could now support a longer period of education for their children and the changing role of the married woman. The role of education in preparing for family life was also examined.

It is only within recent years that reports on education have become best sellers. Indeed, it is probably true to say that it is only recently that teachers themselves in any appreciable numbers have read official reports. Formerly, apart from students of education or those whose work or professional ambitions made it necessary for them to know the contents of reports in detail, most members of the profession were content to read abstracts in the educational journals. Now however it is common to meet not only teachers but also parents who have a fairly detailed knowledge of the contents and recommendations of official reports. The two publications which appear to have roused the greatest parental interest since the war are the Newsom Report[12] and the Plowden Report. This is understandable when one takes into account that these two documents placed a new and strong emphasis on the importance of home/school cooperation. Indeed, Sir John Newsom has said, with regard to the stress placed in the two major reports on the vital need for understanding and cooperation between parents and teachers, 'Indeed I am tempted to say that they made no point more crucial to the future of our schools.[13] In the following chapters frequent reference will be made to the recommendations and findings of these reports, especially insofar as they have special relevance to linking home and school. Mention will also be made of the Seebohm Report,[14] a more recent and less well-known document but one which will probably have far reaching implications both for parents and for teachers.

The Newsom Report was concerned with the education of pupils aged 13 to 16 of average and less than average ability. In his foreword Sir Edward Boyle, then the Minister of Education, pointed out that those who are 'professionally and constitutionally concerned with the work of the schools cannot hope to discover the true needs of these pupils, and the best means of meeting them without the backing of widely informed public opinion.' Although this present book is concerned with almost the whole range of pupils—I have largely excluded discussion of the private sector—there is much in the Newsom Report which is of relevance to all children and their parents. The growth of comprehensive education means that at the secondary level there will be an unprecedented mingling of social and academic groups, and problems that at one time might have been thought to be restricted to only one group will impinge on all. It may come as a surprise to some parents that so many of our young people live and receive their schooling under very primitive conditions, sometimes indeed in an environment of real deprivation. The chapter in the Newsom Report headed 'Education in the Slums' makes for depressing reading but may be a salutary experience for those people who believe that the aims of the Welfare State have already been achieved. Estimates vary but it appears that at least half a million young people in this country live in families where the income is below official subsistence rates. Parents from such families are rarely seen in the school setting unless, as still occasionally happens, an angry father or mother comes to 'have a go' at the teacher. It is worth considering that if teachers and parents are to be real partners in education, then concerned parents may have a part to play in helping the school to make up for the inadequacies of those who either cannot or will not give help to their children. For example, Newsom recommended an extended school day, which for obvious reasons would be of special value to deprived young-sters and which, as will be discussed more fully later, might enable parents to give valuable help in extra-curricular activities and clubs. With regard to general cooperation, paragraph 204 says:

> The schools cannot do the job alone, and parents cannot delegate their responsibility for guiding their children. Many situations would be helped simply by the schools knowing more of the home circumstances and the parent knowing more of what goes on in school. All existing links, such as parent teacher associations, open days, invitations to school functions and concerts, conferences, regular school reports, and most of all, informal conversations between teachers and parents, are extremely valuable/But there is a percentage of homes—and in some districts, a majority—which such arrangements do not touch. In dealing with these problems the schools, and the parents, need special help.

In the three years which intervened between the publication of the Newsom Report and the Plowden Report, the vital importance of a working partnership between parents and teachers was gaining increasing recognition. Indeed, so much emphasis was placed on this partnership in Plowden that detailed references to findings and recommendations will be found throughout this book. In the foreword to the report, written by Anthony Crosland, Secretary of State for Education and Science, the importance of the report for the general public was stressed once again but this time parents were given a special mention. The Secretary of State wrote: 'Their Report is now published and everyone—not only those professionally concerned with education, but parents and the general public—must be grateful for the thoroughness with which they have carried out their task.' Another significant indication of the increasing recognition of the parent can be found in the membership of the committees which produced the two reports—the Newsom Committee were all in one way or another professionally concerned with education or other services for young people, whereas the Plowden Committee list of members shows Mrs M. Bannister, Housewife and Parent, and the Hon Mrs J. Campbell, Housewife and Parent, Hon Secretary, Richmond-upon-Thames Association for the Advancement of State Education.

Plowden acknowledges parents as partners, with a much more than peripheral part to play in the process of education. A whole section of the report is concerned with the 'home, school and neighbourhood' and there is a complete chapter on 'participation by parents'. This chapter begins by stressing the influence of parental attitudes on educational performance and details some of the evidence for believing that one of the essentials for educational advance is a close partnership between teachers and parents. However despite the growing acceptance of the necessity for home/school links, the evidence collected for the Plowden Committee suggests that teachers may be too easily satisfied with their relationship with parents and that there is little factual evidence of any real dissatisfaction about relationships between home and school on the part of many parents. A warning is given that 'This may only be evidence of their low expectations. People tend to accept what they know and do not demand things which they have not experienced.' (paragraph 106)[5] The chapter on participation with parents ends with paragraph 129, which says:

Much depends on the teachers. Every chapter could end thus—but perhaps it is even more apt here than elsewhere. Teachers are already hard pressed, and nowhere more so

21

than in the very districts where the cooperation of parents is most needed and hardest to win. We are aware that in asking them to take on new burdens we are asking what will sometimes be next to impossible. Forty children will seem enough to many, without adding eighty fathers and mothers. Yet we are convinced that to make the effort will not only add depth to their understanding of their children but will also bring out that support from the home which is still often latent. It has long been recognized that education is concerned with the whole man; henceforth it must be concerned with the whole family.

The recommendation that education should be concerned with the whole family finds detailed expression in the Seebohm Report[14] on local authority and allied personal social services. The report covers a wide field but here we will touch upon only those recommendations which concern the subject of this book. Seebohm's main recommendation is the setting up by local authorities of a unified social service department 'providing a community based and family orientated service, which will be available to all'. Among other functions, this department would be responsible for education welfare and child guidance services. Emphasis is placed on community involvement in the social services, especially on cooperation between parents and those services with special responsibility for children. Perhaps the most controversial recommendation so far as educationists are concerned is that made in paragraph 226, which states: 'Social work in schools should be the responsibility of the social service department.' Sir Alec Clegg, Chief Education Officer for the West Riding, has criticized this proposal in no uncertain terms:

> When schools are beginning more and more to question the natural tendency to concentrate on the able and affluent and to look with concern and compassion on the dull and unfortunate, control of the traditional and historic link between home and school is to pass into the hands of a new agency with no experience of educational needs and problems.[15]

Lady Plowden has also stressed that some of the Seebohm

suggestions for increased home/school cooperation may have the opposite effect to that intended, pointing out that if they were adopted it would be necessary to ensure that close contact between home and school is not damaged by the social worker, with his dual responsibility to the head of the school and to the social service department, intervening too frequently. Of special relevance to the next chapter is the recommendation that the new social service department should be given the responsibility for providing, supporting or supervising play-groups for children under five, although two members of the committee found themselves in agreement with the Plowden recommendation that this responsibility should rest primarily with the education department.

References

1  *Report of the Select Committee on the State of Education* (1835)
2  *National Society Monthly Paper* No LII (April 1851)
3  C. K. F. Brown *The Church's Part in Education, 1833–1941* (NSPCK 1942)
4  G. Baron and D. A. Howell *Research Studies 6—School Management and Government* (HMSO 1968)
5  *Children and their Primary Schools* the Plowden Report (HMSO 1967)
6  *The Education of the Adolescent* (HMSO 1926)
7  *The Primary School* (HMSO 1931)
8  *Infant and Nursery Schools* (HMSO 1933)
9  *Secondary Education with Special Reference to Grammar Schools and Technical High Schools* the Spens Report (HMSO 1938)
10  *Early Leaving* (HMSO 1954)
11  *Fifteen to Eighteen* the Crowther Report (HMSO 1959)
12  *Half Our Future* the Newsom Report (HMSO 1963)
13  P. McGeeney *Parents Are Welcome* (Longmans 1969) preface by Sir John Newsom
14  *Report of the Committee on Local Authority and Allied Personal Social Services* the Seebohm Report (HMSO 1968)
15  *Education* vol 132, no 41 (October 1968)

# Chapter 2

# THE UNDER FIVES

Within the world of education there are many who believe that by far the most vital years for the education of the child are— somewhat paradoxically—those which come before the age of compulsory schooling. Within the last decade or so an accumu- lation of research evidence has suggested that the first five years of life, possibly mainly the first two, are of the greatest importance in determining the general direction and setting the probable limits of social, emotional and intellectual development. It appears that a radical change is taking place in official thinking about the relevance for educationists of what happens to the child even before he enters the classroom. Courses for student teachers in colleges or departments of education and the advanced diploma courses provided by institutes of education now place a great deal of emphasis on the study of children's development in the early years. So far as the general public is concerned, the various mass media, especially leading women's magazines and the colour supple- ments of the quality press, offer plentiful information on this topic, often dangerously oversimplified. The BBC programmes on child development also appear to command a large audience. It is a basic premise of this book that despite the difficulties, home/school cooperation should begin in the pre-school years; a wide variety of methods and approaches should be explored so that parents and professional educationists may work together to lay firm foundations.

Almost completely before birth, and normally to a large

extent in the months immediately following, it is the mother who provides the most influential part of the child's environment. The phrase *almost* completely before birth' is used because some external factors can affect the unborn child— dietary deficiencies or illnesses such as German measles for example. Incidentally, a valuable service which teachers could render in discussion with the less well-informed parents is to scotch the numerous folk stories, which are still given credence, about the many weird and wonderful things thought to have an effect on the unborn child. When we move out of the field of folk lore and examine the available evidence for the relative influence of heredity and environmental factors, it becomes more difficult to speak with any certainty, especially as the experts themselves are still far from unanimous on the answer to this old and controversial problem. Much of the heat however has gone out of the 'nature versus nurture' argument, insofar as there now seems to be a fairly broad measure of agreement that both hereditary and environmental factors are important when considering the development of an individual and that any theory which tries to ignore or play down either has no validity. Sometimes, when discussing with groups of parents the concept of the interaction between genetic endowment and environment, I have found it useful to illustrate one aspect of this by a consideration of what are known as critical or sensitive periods in growth. The work of animal behaviourists, such as Konrad Lorenz,[1, 2] has much to teach us here, although there are obvious dangers in attempting to equate the learning processes of one of Lorenz' goslings or ducklings with that of the much more complicated human organism. For an animal a critical period appears to be a time of limited duration which is particularly important for acquiring certain responses. Many psychologists are now of the opinion, based on studies with both animals and humans, that it is a reasonable hypothesis that if the right conditions are not present in the environment when a child is ready to practise some mental or physical function, vital learning may never occur, or occur only with great difficulty at a later date. On the other hand, if the necessary stimulation occurs, learning takes place and the correct responses are established and strengthened. A concept closely allied to that of 'critical periods' is that of 'developmental tasks' or, to use what is probably a more acceptable term, 'optimal learning periods': those stages when a child is ready to walk, talk, perhaps to read or to compute. If he is frustrated then, learning may be blocked. It needs to be emphasized that many psychologists are of the opinion that the importance of 'optimal learning periods' has been overstressed in such publications as the Plowden Report. They point out that a great deal of the evidence is derived solely from experimental work with animals and may in no way be relevant to human behaviour. Certainly it is difficult to prove that some of the same factors apply to human beings as apply to animals. We cannot, for example, deliberately deprive a child of affection or necessary stimulation just to test a theory. Obviously a great deal of research remains to be done in this field but just as obviously the concept of optimal learning periods is of the greatest importance to those who have responsibility for ensuring the healthy growth of the young children in their care.

Further complicating this field of research is the fact that each child is of course unique—a uniqueness arising from the individual interaction between genetic endowment and environmental factors. Even identical twins exhibit marked differences when subjected to differing environments during their growth. All normal human beings do however pass through a fixed sequence of growth and development, a sequence which may be either accelerated or slowed down by favourable or unfavourable environmental factors. This is a common fact of experience so far as physical growth is concerned; rather more uncertainty is found when one comes to consider the evidence for a fixed sequence of emotional or intellectual growth, although there is clearly an association between physical growth and these other aspects of development— aspects which are a great deal more difficult to record and measure. Many parents, while willing to accept that their children's physical growth is partly determined by inherited factors, are not willing to accept the same sort of argument about their children's probable emotional and intellectual development.

The whole topic, especially when discussion takes place between those with an academic knowledge of the subject and parents who, in general, depend on their own experience, arouses considerable argument. Whatever one proposes in theory appears in practice to be contradicted by numerous examples. The child from the almost inarticulate and bookless home who becomes a brilliant academic is as well known as the don's child who converses in grunts and never opens a book. Both teachers and parents have to bear in mind that, despite the claims of the extreme behaviourists, there is no way to forecast with any confidence how an individual's unique genetic endowment will respond to the interplay with the environment. Almost from the moment of birth there is a marked individuality of response and sensitivity. For example, in emotional development it would seem that the ability to deal successfully with stress and frustration depends to a considerable extent on innate factors. Some children seem to be constitutionally more able to tolerate frustration and adversity than others. Nevertheless, the quality of early emotional relationships within the family appears to be of the utmost importance. Children need the security which comes from the unselfish love of members of the family, but they also need stimulation and the opportunity for successful interaction with the world in which they live. 'Smother-love' can be as crippling as lack of affection. The word interaction is a useful one when considering the parent/child relationship, as particularly in the early months of life the giving and receiving of love is a two-way process which may have profound effects on both child and adult. It is the relationship of the infant to his mother or mother substitute that lays the first foundations upon which subsequent emotional, intellectual and social growth is built. This relationship, of course, may be affected by the mother's relationship with other members of the family and one needs to look at the whole family situation when seeking to understand the effect upon the child.

An immensely important contribution to our understanding of the complex interaction between mother and child, and one which has obvious links with the concept of optimal learning periods, is the research carried out by Dr John Bowlby and his co-workers on the effects of maternal deprivation in the early years. In his book *Child Care and the Growth of Love*,[3] a summary of a report prepared under the auspices of the World Health Organization, Bowlby summarizes the evidence of research workers in a number of disciplines, all of whom have come to the conclusion that deprivation in the early years of life is, so far as emotional and intellectual development is concerned, 'equivalent to a vitamin deficiency' in physical growth. A great variety of evidence, both clinical and statistical, points to the general conclusion that a child's health—using that term in its widest sense—depends to a large extent on its early relationships with its mother, varied in countless ways by its relationships with father, brothers and sisters and others in the immediate family.

Since the publication of the reports there has been considerable controversy about the possibility of reversing the effects of severe deprivation by therapy and suitable educational measures. My own view is that we should not too readily accept the hypothesis that if emotional and intellectual potential is stunted in the early years there is little point in taking therapeutic action later on. Some research workers have claimed that although the first five years of life are of crucial importance, behaviour between six and ten years of age is the most closely related to adult personality. This would seem to suggest that experiences during primary school life can modify, to a much greater extent than was once thought possible, later development.

It is a pity that sensational articles in the popular press on the subject of deprivation sometimes cause unnecessary distress to parents. Every child who is hospitalized, or in some other way parted from his mother for a period during the early years of life, is not necessarily going to exhibit signs of deprivation later. Bowlby himself gives an admirable assurance to parents, warning them against giving too much conscious thought to their children's psychological needs. Most mothers need little guidance in providing the love necessary for the growth of emotional security. Where research may help and the professional give useful advice is on the provision of stimulation at the appropriate time so that vital early learning can take place.

28

The normal child's innate curiosity and his desire to explore his environment are characteristics as fundamental as the early clinging response. It is the adult who, like the child in Robert Frost's poem, needs to learn when to hold tightly and when to let go. Not surprisingly, although there have been several attempts, there is no generally accepted classification of children's emotional development and no general consensus of opinion on the growth of the emotions. Psychoanalytical contributions to this subject have been considerable and writers such as Erik Erikson[4] have greatly influenced thinking in this field. However, by their very nature, the contributions of the psychoanalytically oriented writers are difficult, if not impossible, to prove.

Perhaps a more useful approach to development, so far as discussion with parents is concerned, is the work of developmental research workers based on extensive longitudinal observations, such as those of the late Dr Arnold Gesell, of the Mayo Clinic of Child Development, and C. B. Hindley, M. L. Kellmer Pringle and J. W. B. Douglas in this country. Gesell published his first study of child development in 1925 and his scholarly contributions to this field since that date make a most impressive list. A rereading of his writings reminds one yet again how long it takes such valuable insights to reach the stage of general acceptance and to have an influence on child rearing and educational practice. While many people were only paying lip service to the concept that every child is an individual, Gesell and his co-workers were proving the truth of this by carefully documented records. One of Gesell's main contributions was that he helped to abolish the idea that chronological age is of any real importance in determining what we should expect from a child, while at the same time he stressed its importance in giving us our perspectives.

The first part of this chapter is devoted to what may be termed the developmental approach—an approach that is now one of the main strands in modern British educational theory. Because of the increasing emphasis placed on child development, both in official reports such as Plowden and in popular writings on education, parents and teachers will wish to study it more closely.

29

The developmental approach is a two-way process, in which the child teaches and the parent or teacher learns and then, in turn, puts into practice what he has learnt in furthering the education of the child. In no way does it imply pure indulgence but rather a constructive deference to the individuality and limitations of the child. In later chapters we will touch upon how such a complicated concept actually works out in practice, both at the primary and secondary stage. By then it will, I hope, have become apparent that teachers and parents need each other if a true developmental approach is to be used and there is to be any real appreciation of the implications of the wide variance in growth patterns of individuals, and a commonsense acknowledgment of the fact that education can only operate within the limits set by nature. There is some evidence for the view that we delay the progress of our very bright children by not giving them enough to do, but it seems probable that for many more we push them too hard and too fast, thereby laying up trouble for later years. As the great psychologist Claparède, of the Geneva Institute, once wrote: 'You do not imagine that the formation of grown up frogs would be much hastened by cutting off the tail of the tadpole . . . which would probably be done if the frogs had schools.' All this may sound obvious to enlightened readers, but the fact that the Plowden Report practically had to spell out a developmental approach emphasizes that there is still a widespread resistance to the idea that much of the variability of children arises from their biological nature.

In view of the growing interest in child development, it seems likely that many parents would welcome an opportunity for discussion with professional educationists. It is not of course any part of the British educational tradition that teachers, except perhaps those in nursery schools, should have much contact with the parents of pre-school children other than when siblings are involved. It may well be however that in addition to voluntary efforts more discussion groups should be set up as part of the further education provision by local education authorities. In my own authority, Cambridgeshire and the Isle of Ely, many of the village colleges arrange such meetings, and lecturers and teachers are paid as they would be for any other further education activity. Some teachers, especially those who have followed advanced diploma courses and studied the subject in some depth, welcome the opportunity to work in an area which extends beyond their own school's immediate catchment area. If, as suggested in recent official reports, our primary schools become community schools, as indeed many are in my own authority, discussion groups with parents of pre-school children are likely to become much more common. It is relevant that membership lists for the Advisory Centre for Education, an organization which exists to provide information for parents, show that the largest single group among its membership are parents of children not yet at school. One of the difficulties with discussion groups for parents of pre-school children is that they are usually arranged for the evenings, whereas many mothers would find it more convenient to attend during the day. Existing nursery schools and playgroups are obviously suitable places for such discussions and it is probable that the growth in pre-school playgroups will be complemented by a growth in discussion groups for parents. Teachers will inevitably play a large part although other social agencies will have a contribution to make as well. Another difficulty in arranging such groups is that the very children who are to be discussed need looking after. This is why an existing playgroup, nursery or infant school makes an excellent meeting place. The toddlers can themselves be looked after as a group, although there should be no question of immediately parting them from their mothers as soon as they enter the building. It would be poor logic to subject a child to the possibly traumatic experience of sudden parting from its mother while the mother went off to discuss the possibly traumatic experience of a child's first days in a nursery or infant school.

Groups might discuss subjects which are of obvious importance, such as play and language development, but there are also other more immediate topics, such as toilet training, bedwetting, food fads and so on, which are often of great concern to young parents. Some thought might also be given, possibly by local education authorities, to the setting up of groups for those parents of pre-school children who have special difficulties; for example, children who are physically or mentally handicapped, immigrant children and adopted children. As in all attempts to improve home/school relationships there is a danger that unless care is taken it merely becomes a case of preaching to the converted and excluding, by one's actions or by the subjects chosen for discussion, parents from poor social or educational backgrounds. I am fully conscious of the fact that it may be many years before such an approach gains general acceptance in this country but believe that the teaching profession, in addition to rendering a valuable service, may well be able to lessen their own problems at later stages if they extend their interest outside the school gates and down the age groups.

The 1944 Education Act made specific proposals about the provision of nursery education, where desired, for all children of 3 to 5 years. However economic problems and the emphasis placed on improving secondary and further education placed an effective damper on any general provision being made, either as official policy or on the initiative of local education authorities. There were also certain social factors which mitigated against any general or growing demand for pre-school provision.

During the war years many women had been separated from their young children so that they could make their contribution towards the war effort; the day nurseries set up at that time were largely regarded as a temporary, and in no way normal, part of our social life. Possibly because memories of enforced separation between parents and children were so fresh, in the immediate post-war years there was a great deal of heated controversy, even in educational circles, about whether the best place for a child under the age of five years was at his mother's apron or in a nursery school. Certainly in the poorer urban areas there was a fairly widely held feeling that there was a social stigma about trying to get one's child into a nursery; mothers who did so were sometimes made to feel by relations and friends that they were avoiding their responsibilities. Also in the poorer urban areas nursery schools are traditionally regarded as necessary provisions for deprived children rather than a desirable educational provision that pays

32

BAR HILL PLAYGROUP

Home/school cooperation should begin before the children
enter school, as it has in the Bar Hill pre-school playgroup.

Parents and their pre-school children visit a primary school the term before the children enter. They meet the headmistress and teachers and look at the work of the pupils.

both present and later dividends. Perhaps this tradition owes something to the fact that in this country the concern shown by the McMillan sisters for deprived pre-school children first brought nursery education to the public conscience. Nursery education was considered by an official Board of Education Committee as early as 1907 and the conclusions arrived at then coloured the thinking on this subject for many years to come. At that time few people disagreed with the Committee's main recommendation that the best place for a young child was at home unless a poor environment made it necessary to provide nursery schooling. It was recognized however that some nursery schools should be provided, and it was thought that the state system of education was the most suitable agency for making such provision. The 1918 Education Act gave local authorities power to provide nursery education but once again placed stress on the deprived child—an emphasis which no doubt played a significant part in leading the framers of the 1921 Education Act to classify the nursery school as a special school outside the main system of state provision. An official report in the late 1920s showed that only 186,000 children of pre-school age were receiving any education and the great majority of these were attending elementary schools as under-age pupils.

There was little growth in nursery education between the wars but, as we have seen, the 1944 Education Act gave local authorities the power 'for securing that provision is made for pupils who have not attained the age of five years by the provision of nursery schools . . . . or nursery classes in other schools'. However instead of an immediate increase in the nursery provision, the 100% grant to authorities opening day nurseries was ended by the Minister of Health in 1946 and thousands of the day nurseries, opened during the war years to free mothers for work, were closed down. By 1964 there were less than 500 in the whole country. In May 1960, just at a period when the demand for nursery education was beginning to grow, the Minister of Education issued Circular 8/60 which, after some discussion of why the implementation of the 1944 Act with regard to nursery education had failed, stated 'No resources can at present be spared for the expansion of nursery education and in particular no teachers can be spared who might otherwise work with children of compulsory school age.' As Willem van der Eyken points out in *The Pre-School Years*:[5] 'In the entire history of modern British education this is the only case of an actual official embargo being placed on the provision of nursery schooling.' The same author goes on to say that in more than thirty years there has been scarcely any advance in the provision made: 'In March 1932, 5·2% of the under-fives attended either schools or nurseries or their full-time equivalents. In January 1965, it was 7%.'

As we have seen, the official embargo on the provision of nursery education came at a time when, for a variety of reasons, a strong public demand was beginning to be heard. From about 1960 on, this demand grew rapidly and there was a definite swing in educational thinking about the provision which should be made for children under five. Vague phrases about infants being 'better off at their mother's apron' began to be replaced by a much more rigorous examination of the pros and cons of children of all social classes and ability having some form of nursery education. In recent years there is no doubt that the publication of the Plowden and the complementary Gittins Reports,[6] with their emphasis on research findings in child development, has done much to encourage this change of attitude both in parents and in professional educationists. Considerable weight is given in these reports to the argument that the early years are of vital importance.

The emphasis in nursery education is moving away from that of a child-minding, socially therapeutic concern to that of definite educational necessity—the beginnings and, in the opinion of many, the most important part of an educational continuum. Provision for the under fives can no longer be envisaged mainly as a method of removing children from a harsh or deprived environment but as a positive and important stage in the education of all children, be they rich or poor, deprived or indulged.

It is interesting to note that much of the world is way ahead of us in recognizing the importance of provision for the pre-school child. In many continental countries one in three under fives go to nursery school and in Belgium the proportion

34

is as high as two out of three. In the Soviet Union some 45% of town children of pre-school age attend crêches and kindergartens and 10% of rural children do so. Maintained nursery schools in England and Wales can accommodate less than one in a hundred of all eligible children, although the picture is a little brighter in Scotland and Northern Ireland.

In January 1969, members of the Central Advisory Council for Education, who had produced the Plowden Report, issued a press release of the progress which they felt had been made since the report was published. They felt that there were four main spheres in which there had been definite progress. The first of these has already been emphasized, the fact that there is 'a growing interest in and recognition of the importance of the education (in its widest sense) of young children and of the younger children in particular. This interest has been associated with the chapter in the report on children's growth and development and has helped to change considerably the climate of opinion.' The press release then went on to give some examples in support of this claim, beginning with the partial withdrawal of Circular 8/60, saying that this would lead to more teachers and nursery assistants being trained for work with pre-school children, which in turn would bring an increased interest in and knowledge of early childhood. It was pointed out that several colleges of education were now substituting courses for teaching children from 3 to 8 years in place of separate courses for nursery, nursery/infant and infant/ junior work. Other points mentioned were that the National Foundation for Educational Research is conducting an evaluation of pre-school education; the fact that pre-school playgroup membership had quadrupled between 1966 and 1968 and that many authorities now give grants to the two main voluntary bodies concerned with these—the Save the Children Fund and the Pre-School Playgroups Association. This last statement brings us to a consideration of one of the rapid growing points in the provision for the under fives.

Voluntary playgroups

In January 1969 (according to information given in the House of Lords) approval in principle for expenditure amounting to £3½ million was given, under the Government's Urban Aid programme, to 34 selected local authorities. The first phase of the programme provided for 191 new nursery classes with 5,250 full-time additional places (including 21 new nursery schools), 21 day nurseries and some extensions to existing nurseries. In the second phase, involving a larger number of authorities, there is to be an allocation of £4½ million—more than half of it for educational purposes. Approval in principle has been given to the provision of 5,376 additional full-time nursery places and 600 new day nursery places. The Inner London Education Authority has plans to provide nursery education for 90% of their four year olds and half of their three year olds. While such provision will go some way towards meeting the needs in the educational priority areas, it does very little, indeed nothing, to meet the demands now being made by concerned parents in more fortunate parts of the country, who wish for some form of pre-school provision. In fact, the Department's decision to allocate, in the first phase, a large sum to new nursery classes in priority areas was criticized in some quarters because it failed to give a boost to pre-school playgroups run by volunteers. The main argument was that to run a playgroup only costs between a quarter and a third of what is needed to run a nursery class, and the capital costs are far smaller. In the second phase of the Urban Aid programme £150,000 has been allocated to playgroup advisers and societies running voluntary playgroups.

Well before the 1944 Act a number of voluntary organizations were concerned about the need to make provision for the pre-school child. The Nursery School Association was founded in 1923 and in recent years other organizations, such as the Save the Children Fund, have taken a very active part in propagandizing such needs. The playgroup movement appears to have originated from the pioneer work of the New Zealand playgroups begun during the war. In general a playgroup is formed where there are a number of like-minded mothers who are willing to club together and take the initiative in making provision for their children. In this country the Pre-School Playgroups Association was founded in 1962, and in January 1968 its membership stood at 3,000. The vast majority of playgroups are organized by young and intelligent mothers who are anxious to provide a good pre-school environment

36

such as would be available if there were enough nursery schools in existence. Many groups have great difficulty in finding suitable accommodation and must settle for unsatisfactory premises, but inspection by local health departments ensures that no glaring health hazards exist. Usually a small charge is made to parents; the money is used to buy necessary equipment, pay for the hire of premises and pay a trained assistant if the group is lucky enough to find one. Groups have been set up for immigrant children and in recent months a number of hospital groups have been started. In some areas local authority staff help with some form of training.

Perhaps it would be of value to reproduce two comments on a recently formed pre-school playgroup in the village of Bar Hill, near Cambridge. The chairman of the group, Mrs Pamela Lakin, writes:

*Formation*—Discussed by a group of mothers, door-to-door enquiries revealed one hundred per cent support from everyone with children of that age group. A meeting was arranged in a private house for all mothers interested and the secretary of the Cambridgeshire Branch of the Pre-School Playgroups Association came to give a talk on what was involved in running a playgroup. A committee of six was nominated, consisting of a chairman, treasurer, secretary and three members. They had responsibility for the following:

(1) *Preparing a constitution:* A sample constitution used by the PPA was adapted to our own particular needs and adopted at the next general meeting.

(2) *Negotiating for premises:* Difficult, as there was nothing in the way of church hall etc that could be used. Contacted prospective headmaster of the new primary school in the village and invited him to meet the committee. With support from him and cooperation from the local education authority we were able to rent a classroom.

(3) *Raising money:* Difficult. No financial support from any authority and as it was a small, isolated community money raised locally was limited, but the committee

wanted the cost kept down to a minimum so that no child would be prevented from attending due to financial difficulty. Events arranged: several coffee mornings with bring and buy stalls—£10 profit; grand draw with prizes·donated from new shops in the village—£25 profit; dance held at a local factory—£17 profit; stall in Cambridge market selling Christmas toys and decorations made by mothers—£30 profit; developers approached and donated cheque for £25. Taking into consideration the day-to-day running expenses and the amount raised, the committee decided that the lowest economic charge was 2s 6d per year to join the Association and 2s 6d for each attendance, payable one month in advance with no rebate for non-attendance.

(4) *Staffing:* One of the mothers was nursery trained and was willing to run the playgroup and it was agreed to pay her a salary. A rota of mothers was arranged to give her one helper for each session.

(5) *Legal, insurance and other factors involved:* joined PPA and used their insurance scheme giving coverage up to £25,000; applied for permission to run playgroup from local health department; opened a bank account; learnt all about being an employer and what it involved—national insurance stamps etc; applied for registration as a charity to get SET refunded.

*Conclusion:* The playgroup has been a great success. It is held four mornings a week from 9.30 to 11.45 a.m. and has an average attendance of 25 children. Because of the large number of children we can accommodate, the charge of 2s 6d can be maintained in the foreseeable future and this gives a small margin of profit to plough back into funds for buying more equipment etc. We have been able to take some children from outside the village and also to help a boy suffering from severe head injuries after a road accident and give him the stimulation of children of his own age.

Mr W. H. S. Norton, headmaster of the primary school, comments as follows:

The Bar Hill Playgroup has been using the school for a term and a half and it is now possible to take a critical look at the results so far. The group rents a classroom in the school from the county council and this is used for four morning sessions, Monday to Thursday. The mothers formed their own committee and have appointed a qualified nursery assistant to be in charge. Additional help is provided by the mothers via a daily rota system. All the furniture and equipment have been provided by the group and purchased with money raised by coffee mornings, fêtes and other such events. The children come mainly from Bar Hill village, with one or two exceptions, and are all between the ages of three and five. From my point of view as headmaster, the existence of a playgroup gives me an opportunity to see and meet the parents of my future school entrants in a rather informal way. They on the other hand have an opportunity to be aware of what is going on in the school proper, sensing the atmosphere, meeting the staff, seeing the children at work and play during their daily visits. The children themselves benefit from the provision of equipment and opportunities available in the group and also from the fact that they are 'coming to school' like older brothers and sisters. They use the same pegs, wash at the same basins, use the same toilets, and this means that when they are due to transfer to the infant class it will be a natural move into the next room. All the children know our infant teacher and those who will be going into her class after the Easter holidays will have already been into her classroom on several occasions and spent some time with her. The playgroup parents are all invited to our parent teacher meetings and every opportunity is taken to ensure that any difficulties or problems arising in the child's progress and development can be discussed and, as far as possible, dealt with.

The situation described above is to some extent an ideal

one and the fact that Bar Hill is an entirely new village has
obviously shaped the way this particular group has developed.
It is thriving and well established and will probably go from
strength to strength. Though some groups have failed, successful ones are to be found all over the country in both urban and
rural surroundings; their rate of growth is very rapid indeed.
The Pre-School Playgroups Association estimates that by
the end of 1968 there were about 4,000 playgroups in existence.
The majority of these have between 15 and 30 pupils, the
number depending to some extent on whether the group is
held in a hall or a private house. The majority of playgroup
supervisors have some professional qualification, although this
is not so with regard to assistants. Most of the people associated
with playgroups would welcome some further training and
in some areas the local authority's advisory staff help give
them that training. Special appointments have been made in
the form of a salaried playgroup adviser by some authorities
and in others education office staff visit and advise as part of
their normal duties.

Where middle-class and working-class parents join together
to form a playgroup, the middle-class mothers may have a
great deal to give but may also have some adjustments to
make in their thinking. It is mainly the better educated and
articulate parents who initiate playgroups and such people
may be disappointed to find that working-class mothers
approach the activities in a different manner from those who
already have some understanding of children's developmental
needs. It is important that those who seek to help with playgroups recognize that there may be great differences in parental
knowledge. In the past it was perhaps thought necessary only
to encourage parents to teach their children simple toilet
training, washing and the use of the handkerchief, and encourage them to see that their children got the right kind of
food and sufficient sleep, and that they were read stories and
so on. Such information and encouragement are still necessary
for many working-class mothers but some middle-class mothers
would regard it as impertinence for advice from the professionals to be restricted to such matters.

Central to the whole concept of provision for the under fives

40

pre-school provision vital.

is the importance of play. As long ago as the seventeenth century Comenius and John Locke were stressing that knowledge can and should be derived from a wide variety of meaningful, sensory experience. A wide variety of play situations allows for the individual variations in growth and development, but here again we are in a field where we must make most of our judgments on commonsense and observation rather than experimental results. It is not possible to deprive children of play as an experiment, although if we attempt to extrapolate from animal studies we find that when young monkeys have been prevented from social and other play, the consequences have been severe. In human beings, as in animals, play obviously has a biological function and it is in large part a preparation for the more serious business of life which is to follow. The professional educationist may be able to help the inexperienced parents or playgroup assistant in such things as demonstrating how the quality of experience may be more important than the quantity. A good pre-school environment means, of course, outdoor as well as indoor play space. Play areas should be free of dangerous things—old motor cars, for instance, are exciting but may well be dangerous—but at the same time give the children opportunities for adventure. Wherever possible, both indoor and outdoor areas should be such that a wide variety of activities can take place at the same time. Children need room where they can play at being mothers and fathers, places where they can trundle their large toys, wagons, scooters and so on. They need adventure play with boxes, ropes, ladders, bricks, climbing frames, slides and dressing-up materials, and creative play with materials such as sand, paint, water and crayons. Large packing-cases may provide as much opportunity for dramatic play as any expensive Wendy house, as the child's imagination can turn these into space ship, fire engine or a ship at sea in a storm. Children love to take things to bits and put them together again; an old magnifying glass and a broken clock may well provide experience of the utmost value to a young child. Children will also make use of almost anything that will make a musical noise. If water is available they can experiment with plastic bottles, soapsuds, toy boats and so on. If it is possible to keep animals,

41

hamsters and rabbits have always been great favourites.

In both nursery schools and playgroups where good parent teacher relationships have been established, the following examples of cooperation may be found: home visits by the teachers; visits to the school before the child begins, the child accompanying the parents and making the necessary gradual acquaintanceship with the teachers and the building; perhaps a lending library of books and pamphlets which are of use to parents, for example explaining the aims of a developmental approach in the education of young children; regular newsletters or boards for parents' notices. It should not be thought that the fathers have no place in the education of the under fives. Especially in the case of voluntary playgroups they can play a large part not only in making and maintaining equipment but also in giving specialist advice, helping with transport and so on. The nursery school or playgroup is often the first venture of the child into the world outside his own family circle. So far as maintained nursery schools are concerned it may also be the first time a parent has visited an educational establishment since his own schooldays. The high degree of cooperation between the professional leadership and the parents now usually found at the pre-school level may well carry over into the later stages of education.

Most of us judge the stage of development reached by a child by its language growth and it is in this aspect of behaviour that we can really see the value of a good pre-school environment. It is worth stressing that language deprivation may have nothing to do with the economic or social level of the home. The only child of middle-class parents who neglect to talk to him may be far more deprived in this sense than the child from a poor economic background who is surrounded by the constant chatter of brothers and sisters. In general however it appears that the main factor affecting a child's language development is the communication he has with adults in his circle of acquaintances. Parents who take the trouble to explain things and talk to their children in their early years give an advantage that is never lost. As the Newsom Report emphasizes: 'We simply do not know how many people are frustrated in their lives by inability ever to express themselves adequately; or how many may never develop intellectually because they lack the words with which to think and reason.' The report also went on to stress that 'Because the forms of speech which are all they ever require for daily use in their homes and the neighbourhoods in which they live are restricted, some boys and girls may never acquire the basic means of learning and their intellectual potential is therefore masked.' Most of us, whatever our present state of literacy, have at one time or another experienced the frustration which follows the realization that we are unable to express ourselves adequately. Such experiences help us to appreciate, if only in part, the very real problems faced by linguistically deprived boys and girls the moment they step outside their normal environment. There are many research findings[7, 8] which point to the fact that children from working-class homes do less well at all levels of education than comparable contemporaries from middle-class homes, mainly because of linguistic distinctions. Professor Basil Bernstein of the University of London Institute of Education, has probably done more than any other British research worker to underline the fact that wide chasms still exist in this country because of language differences.[9] Bernstein has emphasized that in the past we have tended to oversimplify the problems associated with changing or improving the spoken language of children from poor backgrounds and he has shown that in certain areas sheer inarticulateness is less of a problem than the contrast between the different languages of home and school. At the same time he points out that verbal impoverishment represents only one aspect of an individual's range of potential responses, and that it is mainly in the artificial and formal setting of school that this impoverishment works to the pupil's disadvantage. He has categorized the lower working-class, which he estimates at about 29% of the population, as in general a section of society where children have very little intercommunication with adults and are, therefore, linguistically disadvantaged, although he carefully points out that 'there is, of course, a wide range of individual differences.' He further warns that such disadvantage 'will not be found with all children of the particular social background' to which he refers. One of the most marked differences between the privileged and deprived child is that linguistically disadvantaged children are limited in their ability to plan or organize verbally and are in consequence more rigid thinkers than those from an enriched environment.

This last sentence brings us to what is perhaps the most important single concept in the new emphasis which is at present being placed on provision for the under fives. Until fairly recently it was generally accepted by most professional educators, if not by parents, that intelligence was innate and that little could be done to change or improve whatever mental capacity it is that is measured by testing. Now however it is generally recognized that the early years are vital so far as the growth of intelligence is concerned.

Without doubt improved educational provision for all our children under the age of five would produce a more intelligent population. It has been demonstrated pretty conclusively that where changes in the development of intelligence take place, 50% of this happens before the age of four and a half,[10] and Dr W. D. Wall, Dean of London University Institute of Education, is quoted as saying that a pound spent before four is probably worth twenty pounds spent after the age of eight.

This book is not the place to enter into argument in depth about the relative importance of genetic endowment and environmental factors, but it is emphasized once again that what we describe as intelligence is developed by the continuous interaction of the environment and the genetic inheritance. At the present there is little one can do about genetic inheritance, although there are hopeful signs that science may soon devise some method of righting genetic defects. Environment however is subject to some manipulation, although the Plowden Report was perhaps overoptimistic in this respect. As Basil Bernstein and others have pointed out, well-staffed schools in slum areas may not really get to the root of the problem, and sometimes there are wrong-headed attempts to improve children's intellectual and linguistic development; for example, when too much is expected of a sudden transfer of working-class children to middle-class play situations.

To a large extent intelligence would appear to be a self-fulfilling prophecy—what the culture and environment lead the child to expect that he will grow into. This is why it is vital for parents and teachers to work together even at the preschool phase. Parental attitudes are of the utmost importance and remain so throughout the child's school life. As the National Survey made for the Plowden Committee showed, variations in parental attitudes can account for more of the differences in children's school achievement than either the variation in home circumstances or the variation in schools. A striking fact that we should constantly bear in mind when assessing how much emphasis should be placed on improving home/school relationships.

### References

1 K. Lorenz *King Solomon's Ring* (Methuen 1952)
2 K. Lorenz *On Aggression* (Methuen 1966)
3 J. Bowlby *Child Care and the Growth of Love* 2nd edition (Penguin Books 1965)
4 E. H. Erikson *Childhood and Society* revised edition (Norton 1963)
5 W. van der Eyken *The Pre-School Years* (Penguin Books 1967)
6 *Primary Education in Wales* the Gittins Report (HMSO 1967)
7 J. W. B. Douglas *The Home and School* (MacGibbon and Kee 1964)
8 J. W. B. Douglas *All Our Future* (Peter Davis 1968)
9 B. Bernstein 'Social Structure, Language and Learning,' Chapter 6 in *Linking Home and School* Craft, Raynor and Cohen (eds) (Longmans 1967)
10 B. Bloom *Stability and Change in Human Characteristics* (Wiley 1964)

# Chapter 3

# BEGINNING THE PARTNERSHIP

The claim is often made (although mainly by British educationists) that the infant schools of this country are the best in the world. Certainly so far as the education of the children of the poor is concerned, it is the infant schools which have the longest history and it is in these schools that many of the progressive innovations—subsequently adopted at later stages of education —have been tested and proved.

In 1819 the first purpose-built infant school was established in Westminster under the direction of James Buchanan, a teacher who had worked in Robert Owen's pioneer school in New Lanark. Other infant schools were set up in Spitalfields, Bristol and Walthamstow and, following the formation of the Infants' School Society in 1825, the movement spread rapidly —until within twenty years the country had at least 500 infant schools.

The Plowden Report states that the choice of five as the age at which children must begin school was made almost by chance in 1870; in fact by the time of the 1870 Education Act, infant schools were firmly established and became an integral part of our system of state education, a system which has a compulsory age of entry lower than almost anywhere else in the world. In most countries, with the exception of Israel and a few states whose educational systems derive from ours, compulsory schooling begins at the age of six.

A contemporary description of one of the early infant schools reads:

They depend not on discipline but on maintaining the interest of the children. The system is designed to be pleasurable to infants at every step. Lessons are to be formed into verses: they are said to measured time . . . periods of learning are short and frequently changed. There are periods of play in the playground with footballs, hoops, swings and ropes.

This is in some way similar to the description one might write of a good infants' school in the late 1960s. Unfortunately, the progressive start made by the early infants' schools was not maintained and almost everywhere the education of even the youngest children became formal in the worst sense of that term. In the nineteenth century few progressive innovations were actually begun in this country, although attempts were made to introduce some of the ideas of the educational reformers. The Home and Colonial Infant School Society was founded in 1836 and one of the main aims of this organization was the training of infant teachers in the ideas of the Swiss educationist Pestalozzi. In 1875 the Froebel Society for the Promotion of the Kindergarten System was formed. At this stage in our history both Germany and America were well ahead of us in the education of young children and in some measure the ideas of the early Continental reformers, even those of Rousseau, reached us in a refined form after considerable trial in the United States. The education of young children owes much to the genius of Rousseau and the putting into classroom practice of his apparently simple but revolutionary developmental concepts, such as 'nature would have children be children before being men' and 'childhood has its own ways of seeing, thinking and feeling.' Both quotations are from his treatise on education, *Émile*.[1]

By the second decade of the twentieth century, as Plowden points out: 'A considerable body of liberal thinking on the education of children was available to teachers. Rousseau, Pestalozzi, Froebel, Whitehead, Dewey, Montessori and Rachel McMillan, to mention only a few, had all written on lines that encouraged change and innovation.' In the years between the wars the psychoanalytic schools also had considerable influence.

Freud, Jung and Adler all contributed to the growing literature on the education of the young child. Pioneer schools, such as that of Susan Isaacs at the Malting House in Cambridge, showed that a progressive child centred education was possible in practice as well as theory. The Plowden Report doubts however whether the educational reformers mentioned above had any great influence on British infant teachers, but claims 'Perhaps the strongest influence was that of Froebel, mediated through the Froebel Training Colleges which bore his name.'

My own opinion is that the American philosopher, John Dewey, also made a significant contribution at this time to our thinking about education at the infant and junior stages. Dewey placed his main emphasis on encouraging the ability to think and believed that the ability to reason is developed by children through active attempts at problem solving.[2] Considerable research evidence now exists for this belief.[3] Progressive educationists, concerned with work at the primary level, generally accept problem solving as a principal educational objective, although as Professor Paul H. Hirst has pointed out there are many dangers in considering 'problem solving' as 'a principal educational end' rather than just as 'one possible objective to be considered along with many others'.[4] As touched upon in a previous chapter, play is largely a problem-solving activity; although Comenius was preaching this as early as the seventeenth century, the contention that play is of the utmost value so far as young children are concerned still seems to be regarded with suspicion in some quarters. For example, in a recently published book *Perspectives on Plowden*,[5] Professor Brian Foss, of Bedford College, University of London, writes:

> In several places (e.g. pp 193 and 201) the report empha-
> sizes the importance of play and the value of 'discovery'
> methods. The authors may be right, but it should be
> pointed out that there is little evidence regarding what
> the importance and value are. Most children play, and
> most of the time they are playing they appear to be pre-
> occupied, and often happy, which is rewarding for the
> teacher. However it is impossible to find out experimentally
> what would happen to a child who is not allowed to play.

Mothers are welcome to stay in the classroom during the first day of school.

Parents can help to build an adventure playground like this one. A few hours of work by parents can give many hours of pleasure to children.

It is worth spending some time on Dewey's ideas as they are having a renewed and growing impact on British educational thought at all levels. As already indicated, Dewey believed that children can be taught to think and that a true education consists of the full development of curiosity and habits of exploring and testing—a process he described as 'the method of intelligence'. It was in the late twenties and early thirties that progressive education at the primary stage along the lines advocated by this great educationist really began to catch the minds of a number of British teachers. As the movement spread many critics felt that the pendulum had swung too far and that traditional teaching of the 'essentials' was being ignored. In some cases perhaps there was cause for concern since some of the more unreflective enthusiasts, in their misunderstanding of what was being asked of them, provided valuable ammunition for the 'back to the essentials' school of thought—a situation somewhat similar to the growth in the late 1960s of what has been termed 'educational backlash'. For example, at the conference of the Conservative National Advisory Committee on Education held in London in June 1969, a Leicestershire secondary school headmaster proposed a motion welcoming 'the changing emphasis from teaching to individual learning' and 'the establishment in our schools of an enriched educational atmosphere in which children may develop their own unique potential'. The conference however rejected the motion by a two to one majority. Opposing the motion, the headmaster of a London comprehensive school said, 'Free expression means 30 children gibbering nonsense.' It is a depressing thought that such a motion should be rejected in this day and age; one can only hope that the unreflective panic which appears to have been caused by the publication of the recent *Black Papers*[6] will be temporary in its effect. Extremists, on both the right and the left, tend to obscure the real issues.

It is true that some practices carried out in the name of progressive education deserve to be condemned. There are probably still schools where 'activity' or 'choosing time' is shown as a period on the time-table and mainly consists of unstructured and unsupervised play with clay, jigsaws, construction toys and so on, even for intelligent top junior boys and girls. This is hardly problem-solving education as Dewey envisaged it.

Dewey has a special claim for a place in this book as it was he who first stated: 'What the best and wisest parent wants for his children that must the community want for all its children.' The rub comes, as will be touched upon more than once in the following chapters, when we attempt to define what is meant by 'the best and wisest parent'. As I have discussed in some detail in another publication,[7] head teachers sometimes find that when they attempt to introduce progressive ideas into their schools it is the articulate, ambitious parents, with children in the examination forms, who are their greatest critics. Certainly my own experience leads me to believe that it is from middle-class homes, often the homes of university teachers, that the severest attacks are made on progressive methods in local authority schools. Professor Ayer, himself a member of the Plowden Committee, has gone to some trouble to explain in a press article why he is buying a private education for his children. This is perhaps a typical example of those who advise, legislate and administer our state system but choose to send their own offspring to traditional private schools. It is important to remember that the value aspirations and orientations of middle-class and working-class parents may be poles apart. Working-class parents may be, and often are, more concerned with the all-round development of their children, even though this may be expressed as 'just so long as he's happy,' while the majority of middle-class parents, somewhat understandably, are more concerned about levels of attainment in academic subjects and examination successes. Fear that the comprehensive schools may be 'captured' by ambitious, middle-class parents to the detriment of the non-academic boy and girl has its origin in this situation.

Professor John Barron Mays, in a contribution to *Headship in the 1970s*,[8] makes a similar point when he writes:

There is a danger then that the sophisticated and often pushing parents of established middle-class backgrounds will have an undue influence on what goes on in the school, dominating the Parents' Association and putting pressure on the teachers, while the more diffident and socially more self-conscious and self-effacing parents from traditional working-class backgrounds will leave too much to the school and avoid interfering in its policies and affairs.

As we have seen, the majority of the nation's children who will begin school at the age of five or just before will have had no experience of organized education. From the beginning of compulsory education the problem of transfer appears—a problem which will recur at various stages throughout the child's educational career. At first it is the problem of transfer from home to school and the Plowden Report gave a great deal of attention to this subject. For example, it was suggested that admissions to the infants' school should be staggered over half a term so that each child and each child's mother could be separately welcomed and made to feel at home. At the time of the national survey made for the Plowden Committee in 1963, a third of the schools involved 'did not expect their new children all to start school on the first day of term—twelve schools spent three days in welcoming the newcomers, four spent over a week and nine a fortnight or more. Another six said five year olds were free to join any day of the term they became five, and four that children entered in the week of their fifth birthday.' This last system is obviously a thorough form of staggering. The report went on: 'But welcoming a child is more than a matter of reserving proper time to attend to him. It is the quality of the welcome and the imaginative insight given to it which counts.' Further it said:

The kind of things that impressed the inspectors, and they seem right to us, were invitations to mothers and children to spend some time in the children's first class before admission, encouragement to mothers to stay with children who are anxious during the first few days at school, welcoming letters to parents with suggestions on how to help their children to make a successful start, and meetings for discussions between the school staff and the parents of five year olds.

Even where a child has previously attended a nursery school there may be some difficulties at the stage of transfer to compulsory schooling, as a single nursery school may send its children to a number of different infant schools. Some nursery heads are attempting to ease this problem and some of their methods are described in the Inner London Education Authority booklet *Home and School*,[9] which says:

> When the time of transfer approaches, the head of the nursery may take groups of children on a morning visit to their infant school. The parents are told of the visit whose purpose is to introduce the children to the new building, explore the reception class and if possible meet the reception class teacher in whose care they will be. This preliminary visit is followed by another, arranged by the nursery head, when the individual child is taken by his mother to meet the head of the infant school. It is helpful too if the infants' reception class teacher can visit the nursery and meet the children again in an environment where they are at home. Any helpful background information about the child or his home should be passed on at this stage or later to the infants' head. After transfer, the head of the nursery school may visit the infants' school to see how her children are settling in and this further contact and opportunity to discuss the children's progress with infant colleagues can be mutually rewarding.

In 1968 the Department of Education and Science published Education Survey No 5 *Parent/Teacher Relations in Primary Schools*.[10] This survey was a direct result of a recommendation made in the Plowden Report to the effect that the Department should 'issue a booklet containing examples of good practice in parent/teacher relations'. Chapter 2 deals with 'Entry and Transfer' and begins:

> Infant and junior mixed and infants' schools are usually larger than nursery schools, and relationships with parents are consequently a little harder to achieve. Some schools find that vertical grouping, either for the whole age range of the infant school or for a narrower age span, makes it easier for parents and children to feel at home in the school.

More will be said about vertical grouping as a form of organization later in this chapter.

In the survey examples are given of schools which arrange introductory visits, and the majority view appears to be that such visits should take place at least half a term before the beginning of full-time schooling. A school is described where the first approach is by letter, which, after telling the parents that a place will be available for their child, invites them to come along and meet the class teacher and the head on three separate occasions. On each visit both parent and child grow more accustomed to the school and the school routine. During the first visit, along with ten or twelve other children, the parents stay with the child and the group follows normal infant activities, ending the visit with a story told by the teacher. This first introduction lasts for an hour; on the second occasion the child is left in the group without the parent for an hour, and this procedure is repeated at the third visit. While the children are in classrooms the parents are encouraged to go to the staffroom and have a cup of tea and a chat with the head teacher.

The survey describes another school with an even more ambitious programme. Mothers and children are invited to attend one afternoon a week for a whole term before the children start. The headmistress of this school also visits the homes of her new pupils in the holidays before they enter. Some schools find an open evening, which fathers as well as mothers can attend, useful in the term before entry. A growing number of heads, in addition to encouraging visits, send a letter or issue simple booklets about their schools, giving information about aims and organization and perhaps giving advice about how parents can help their child both in preparation for school and once he is in attendance. An excellent example is given in the survey of such a letter, which was drafted by a head in consultation with parents, who were able to help him emphasize the points which they felt to be the most important. This letter suggests ways in which parents can reassure their child on his first entry to school, how they can help with school work and what help is most appropriate at this age.

The survey describes another school, which arranges for

parents to meet teachers early in the first term as follows:

After about a month each new parent is invited, by name, to visit the school for a coffee morning. The children come into school at the normal time and the parents are invited for about 10.0 a.m. When the mothers arrive they are given a name label, which they are asked to pin on as much to get to know other mothers as for the benefit of the staff. The programme includes a music and movement lesson which helps the parent understand the need for children changing into appropriate dress and particularly for working in bare feet. The parents may go into any of the classrooms and the headmistress and the teachers answer questions about what is going on. Coffee and biscuits are served during the children's playtime and parents may talk over what they have seen together with members of the staff. One of the classrooms is then set up with a slide projector and screen. The headmistress shows a series of slides of activities that go on in the school, and explains in straightforward language the educational implications. At some time during the morning the parents are also taken into the school kitchen; the mothers find this of particular interest for this is a school where more than 82% of the children stay for school meals. Both mothers and fathers—a few of them manage to come—join in the normal school assembly.

The end of this particular section of the booklet gives an interesting example of the practical application of research results when it states:

It is not unusual for summer born children, who are at a disadvantage in many ways, to be excluded until the term following their fifth birthday because the schools are already full. Some schools have tried to reduce their disadvantage by arranging a sequence of afternoon meetings with the mothers, who are shown various kinds of play material and given advice on story telling and the use of books.

Great stress has been placed in preceding chapters on the

importance of parents, as well as teachers, gaining an understanding of developmental trends in young children and it has been suggested that as early as possible many parents would welcome some insight into child development, especially in the areas of behaviour and school achievement. Parents sometimes worry about their child's achievement, even in subjects which they do not regard as important basic skills—for example, a parent may be concerned over his youngster's apparent lack of imagination in drawing. By the age of five a child has usually developed his own idiom for such objects as trees, birds, houses and so on, and parents get annoyed by the fact that the boy or girl often wants to draw the same thing over and over again. This reluctance to change skills which have been mastered or proved successful in the past is a trait which is well known to all experienced teachers and one of their principal tasks is a skilful leading of the child to new levels of interest and achievement.

An important fact, almost impossible to overstress, is that in this country the majority of parents make their first contact with the teacher when their child enters the infant school. It is at this stage that some parents desperately need advice and it is often here that help and advice are most welcomed. The examples of good practice, such as those described in this book, are by no means widespread, yet it is at the time of entry to the infant school that parents' attitudes to school may be set for a long time, perhaps for the rest of their child's formal education. One of the main factors which will influence parents' later attitudes is their initial encounter with their child's teachers. It is perhaps difficult for the ordinary middle-class teacher to appreciate just how much faith and trust a working-class mother may place in her child's teachers until something happens to disturb or dispel that faith. Parent/teacher cooperation is desirable at all levels of education but it is of vital importance in the education of children of working-class parents, where right from the beginning teachers and parents need to rely on and trust each other.

In general, fortunately, teachers of infants are good ambassadors for our system of education. Even so, it may be difficult for the older infant teacher to appreciate that the parents of today's infants—sometimes themselves the product of an

55

enlightened education—are in most cases very different from those she was likely to meet at the beginning of her career. Monica Furlong, writing in the *Teacher's World* for 13th September 1968, has this to say about her own child's introduction to school:

> Most significant of all, and most traumatic for parent and child, is the method of starting school which consists more-or-less of bundling a five year old through the door and leaving him to it. Mother and child have spent the five previous years in the closest possible communication. Except in rare cases this union cannot be suddenly sundered without pain to the child, so that what is frequently asked of a mother is a deliberate infliction of pain and a betrayal of trust. 'Mummy is just going out to do some shopping,' said a teacher to my weeping child, murmuring to me *sotto voce* to get the hell out. The only possible response seemed to be to tell her that my child and I did not have that sort of relationship. We were accustomed to telling one another the truth (and, I might have added, to not leaving members of our family to strangers at moments when they were distraught with unhappiness).[11]

Earlier in this chapter it was pointed out that Education Survey No 5 said that some schools found that vertical grouping made it easier for parents and children to feel at home in the school. Certainly as an increasing number of schools move over to this form of organization, it has provided a valuable opportunity for heads and staff of infant schools to explain to parents just what they believe the aims and objectives of infant education should be.[12] Some parents will perhaps remember the criticisms directed at small rural schools in their own young days and will find the concept of vertical grouping a difficult one to understand. They are often unhappy at the thought of their child spending the whole of his or her infant school life with the same teacher; this may be especially true where 'going up' into a new class has become associated in the minds of some parents, and children, with the final step towards the junior school, or with better discipline or more emphasis on the basic skills. Balanced against this is the greatly increased opportunity for parents and teachers to get to know each other really well in a manner which may not be possible again for the rest of the child's school career.

So far we have concentrated mainly on methods of providing information for parents about what actually happens in the schools. This is an established and well tried method of drawing parents into partnership. A more revolutionary suggestion, and one which to date has not been greeted with a great deal of enthusiasm by most teachers, is that which proposes that parents might give practical help with their children's education actually within the school itself. As with so many other aspects of home/school relationships, a great deal of pioneering work along these lines has already been carried out in the United States, where, for example, many schools have long had a rota system of class mothers, whose main duties are to relieve the teachers of extraneous responsibilities. At the time of writing, comparatively few schools in this country actually encourage parents to make a practical contribution within the school setting, although the idea is gaining ground rapidly in both infant and junior schools. It would be as well to acknowledge immediately that it is asking a lot for British teachers to revise completely their view of the accepted and traditional roles of parents and teachers. The new concept demands that the profession accept that it is no longer sufficient to think of school as a community consisting solely of pupils and teachers. There is considerable resistance to this view; for instance, at the Annual Conference of the National Association of Head Teachers, held at Blackpool in May 1969, a motion was proposed calling for caution over parent participation in school life. In proposing this motion, a speaker said, 'We are being forced into the situation where parents will be led to think they have a right to take a part in the running of the school. Instead, I would like parents to feel a little honoured if they are invited into the school.' However, another delegate spoke strongly against the motion and accused his colleagues of 'a timid apprehensiveness about parents whereas they ought to be able to make effective use of the parent teacher associations'. The motion was in fact carried by a large majority— again underlining the fact that teachers are no more likely to change established habits and attitudes overnight than any other group of people. It would be naïve to think that sweeping changes will occur rapidly.

The types of activities described in the following pages are by no means common; but there are some hopeful indications that once parents are accepted and welcomed into a school as active participants in their children's education, other schools in the locality quickly follow suit. As has happened so often in the development of our educational system, it is mainly in the infants' schools that experiments on a large scale are being carried out with these progressive ideas and also, as so often before, it is likely that these ideas will eventually be adopted by later stages of education.

Before any real advance will be made, the main factor inhibiting necessary experiment must be overcome. This factor is the basic psychological attitudes of both parents and teachers in this country—attitudes which have been shaped both historically and socially by very powerful forces indeed. It would be unwise to underestimate their strength. There are many parents who find it is difficult enough to attend even a large parent teacher meeting, where, if they wished, they could remain anonymous. Such parents would find it impossible, without a great deal of encouragement, to enter the school as an active partner in their own child's, or indeed other children's, education. Some working-class men would think it unmanly to show an interest in the school, and it would not do to underestimate working-class attitudes towards those of their numbers whom they regard as toadying or currying special favours for their children. Teachers, perhaps especially if they come from a working-class background themselves and have been teaching for some time, may find the whole idea of parents actually working in the school so strange and so disturbing that they can hardly bring themselves to consider such a proposition seriously.

However, parent participation has always been common in the youth club movement which, right from the beginning, took account, as did the uniformed organizations, of parental interests and enthusiasm; the concept is not therefore as novel as it might at first seem. Increasingly, young parents have themselves attended schools where modern methods were the rule and where relationships between children, parents and staff were friendly, cooperative and uninhibited.

Our system of compulsory education has in the past placed much emphasis on parental rights and obligations. Progressive educationists welcome the indication that in future the emphasis will be on parental cooperation and participation. Almost since the introduction of compulsory education the majority of parents in this country have shown an astonishing degree of confidence in teachers, allowing them not only to teach the basic skills but also to inculcate their own individual educational philosophy. Parents are confident that, although teachers differ in their approach to the profession, they will always put the interests of their pupils above all other considerations. It would seem that the time is coming when this goodwill and trust should be reciprocated—the teaching profession should begin to show confidence in parents. So far as education is concerned we are living in an age of rising expectations by both parents and teachers. A real partnership is one of the ways in which we can ensure that such expectations are realized.

We have looked at some of the possible reasons why this country has allowed parents to be neglected for so long and so consistently. In some ways it is difficult to understand why this has happened, especially as in so many respects Britain has taken the lead in the field of public education. Certainly, in some of the English-speaking countries overseas, such as Rhodesia, parents are expected to take an active and practical part in the education of their children. Even on the financial side much greater demands are made on parents than here, although in Britain supplementary fund-raising activities are as old as compulsory education itself. An entry for 1895 in the Willingham Infants' School, Cambridgeshire, logbook reads: 'A wall museum bought with concert money and looks very nice.' Today such a museum might be far more ambitious and consist of a separate building erected, stocked and, to some extent, staffed by the parents. Fund-raising to supplement equipment is of course an important part of parental involvement, especially in times of fairly strict economy, and there seems little doubt that in the years to come parents will increasingly dig their hands into their pockets. However the remainder of this chapter will not be concerned with fund-raising activities but with an examination of some of the methods of giving practical help which might be attempted by parents at the infant stage of education. It will be clear that many of the suggestions and activities could apply equally well to other age levels.

To deal with one of the more obvious objections about parental participation in educational priority areas first—what can a parent, who is poorly educated and not financially well off, do to help? Working-class parents *do* have skills which would be of immense help if intelligently utilized by the schools. Certainly, when one considers the actual physical condition of many of our schools, it seems that much greater use could be made of the practical skills of parents. Michael Young, himself a pioneer in the field of home/school relationships, has pointed out: 'Most working people will only feel self-confident in the school if they feel they have something to contribute to it. Many of them are proud of the work they do with their hands. How can they bring this asset to the service of the school?'[13] Characteristically Young encouraged experiment to find an answer. For example, the Institute of Community Studies initiated a project in some London schools where parents not only made normal visits to see the children at work but really became involved in a practical way—they painted, mended and sewed, using their practical skills to brighten up the school and in this way expressed their sense of identity with the school. This occurred in areas which only a few years ago would rarely have seen a parent inside a school unless the purpose of the visit was to make a complaint.[14] Patrick McGeeney gives many examples of such practical help in *Parents Are Welcome*.[15] If ordinary parents are to go into their children's school for the express purpose of making a contribution rather than a complaint, there are many forms such a contribution might take. There appear to be two main categories of practical help that parents can offer—helping in the classroom, and organizing or assisting with out-of-school activities. Let us first consider the type of practical help where parents put into use some of the skills they possess. Village schools have a tradition of calling upon fathers to make and repair toys, especially the large push-and-pull or building toys so beloved by the younger children. Wendy houses too are expensive to purchase but easy to build. Most schools these days have some sort of activities allowance, even if no extra school fund; if the school supplies the materials, and the labour and skill are forthcoming from parents, no infant classroom need be without important pieces of equipment.

There are practical problems in such a suggestion. Materials may be available, volunteer labour freely offered, but workshop facilities, where a group may work (and the group contribution is an important part of parent participation) may be non-existent. Two possible answers are worth considering: a local secondary school may provide the necessary woodwork and metalwork facilities, or a group of parents could actually build and equip a combined parents' workshop and discussion room. This building could double for use by the children. The latter is certainly a more imaginative answer to the problem. Obviously such a project would need the consent and very often the help and advice of County Hall staff, but such projects have been successfully carried out and there seems little reason why they should not become as much a commonplace of parental involvement as have learner swimming pools during the last few years. Although I have used the term 'group of parents' above, obviously the greatest benefit to all concerned is when the group for such an activity consists of parents, teachers and pupils.

Groups of parents have also provided primary schools with climbing and other agility apparatus, sand pits and adventure playgrounds. (A simple adventure playground may consist of little more than a mound of earth and a few simple balancing blocks; a complex one can be a real wonderland, complete with tunnels, complicated climbing frames and even concrete ships and fire engines.) Most infant and junior schools could make good and continued use of a pond in their grounds for pond-dipping expeditions, and parents can not only dig and construct such a pond but also help to keep it stocked with the myriad things that so fascinate young children. Pond-dipping, incidentally, is one of those activities where mothers might help with supervisory duties. The growing use of the family grouping form of organization makes such help invaluable, and although most schools now have paid ancillary helpers there is always room for several other pairs of hands, ears and eyes. Some years ago only a few infant classrooms had animals, some perhaps a solitary guinea pig. Schools are now much more ambitious and a wide variety of animals are kept. These animals obviously need a great deal of attention; it is a valuable educational experience for the children themselves to be made as responsible as possible for them, but sometimes there are jobs to be done which are beyond the capabilities of the six or seven year old, however willing. The modern trend is to keep animals in verandas attached to the school—an enthusiastic building group could undertake to build these verandas.

Those parents who, for one reason or another, cannot help in heavy building tasks such as constructing a swimming pool or a parents' workroom, might well be willing to give assistance with some of the lighter but necessary construction jobs, such as making and erecting library shelves or display boards.

Some mothers might find it very difficult to help in the school library but could cope successfully with a group taking part in one of the most valuable of all educational situations for young children—a baking session round the school stove. One mother might be of great help in supervising children at a school party or helping with the food, but assisting with the savings money might be quite beyond her. On the other hand, such necessary and important help as dealing with handicapped pupils, perhaps even just helping them about the school (and depending on local policy, physically handicapped children are often found in ordinary schools) is something that almost all mothers are capable of doing. (This present book is not the place to discuss parents' participation in the junior training centres for severely subnormal children but recent personal experience leads me to believe that here is an area where unpaid ancillary help is desperately needed.) In the infant school, especially at the reception stage, children spend much of their time in play and if they are to get the full educational benefit from their play experiences they need friendly and helpful adult supervision. With the growth of learner swimming pools, just the sheer task of ensuring that the toddlers are properly dried and dressed has become immense, and the tying of shoelaces or putting on and taking off outer garments and wellingtons on wet days, is a time-consuming chore that only those who have given help in infant classrooms can really appreciate.

Other activities where parents have assisted are classifying and repairing school books, helping with the teaching of musical instruments and making and showing films. This last item is a reminder that one of the factors working against the introduction of educational technology, especially in the infant school, is the feeling of inadequacy that many teachers of young children have when faced with the wide range of audiovisual equipment now available. For example, with the introduction of vertical grouping there is an obvious place for taped stories —perhaps with slides—that are heard by a small group of children or even an individual child. Many a teacher of infants is skilled at telling stories but would hesitate to attempt to tape one, let alone make slides to go with it. Building up a library of such stories and servicing and adapting the necessary equipment is something that might well be undertaken by interested parents.

An increasing number of women now drive and many have the use of a car; providing transport for special occasions is an obvious and useful way of giving practical help to a school. For instance, sometimes it is necessary to take a child to hospital—this usually means that the head or a member of staff has to leave the school and wait, perhaps for two or three hours, while the patient is being attended to. Parents could provide a rota of driver mothers ready to help in such emergencies.

Making collections of pictures, duplicating, typing, tending the school garden, collecting junk for model making, helping with the actual model making, stocking dressing-up boxes and making costumes—these are all time-consuming activities, sometimes demanding special skills, with which many teachers would welcome assistance once they have accepted the initial idea of parents helping in a really practical manner.

As we have seen, some members of the profession will dismiss activities such as those discussed above as hopelessly idealistic.

No doubt they would view with horror the prospect of an increase in parental participation which, in their view, must inevitably lead to interference by non-professionals on a grand scale. One might hope that these teachers would consider such factors as the obvious impossibility of giving enough of the necessary attention to classes of forty or more infants. In present day infants' schools there are just not enough adults to go round. Ample research findings point to the fact that young children need continuous contact with adults, with whom they can converse and whom they can involve in their activities. My own experience as an inspector has shown me how welcome another adult is in the infant classroom, both to teachers and to the children, who are desperately anxious to show their work and be given encouragement and approval. Mention of my own visits reminds me that infant children welcome the presence of men in the classroom, possibly because a good infant classroom is in many ways an extension of the home. It is odd that there should be a resistance to the idea of men in the infant school when one remembers that most of the great educational reformers who have influenced the development of progressive education in the infant school have been males.

A father or mother who helps in the classroom may have much to give a receptive teacher. The enlightenment that follows parent/teacher cooperation is a two-way process. I have suggested elsewhere that each classroom should contain a notice 'Remember, the teacher could be wrong.'[16] Perhaps each school staffroom should have a notice on the wall saying 'Remember, the parent could be right.' Where a parent is right all the children may benefit, and parents are beginning to realize that ensuring good conditions for their own children means that they must also try to ensure good conditions for all children.

# References

1 J. J. Rousseau *Émile* (Everyman Library)
2 J. Dewey *How We Think* (D. C. Heath 1933)
3 E. A. Peel *Programmed Thinking* (Programmed Learning, July 1967)
4 Schools Council *Working Paper No 12: The Educational Implications of Social and Economic Change* (HMSO 1967)
5 R. S. Peters (ed) *Perspectives on Plowden* (Routledge and Kegan Paul 1969)
6 C. B. Cox and A. E. Dyson (eds) *Fight for Education—A Black Paper* and *Black Paper Two* (Critical Quarterly Society 1969)
7 R. G. Cave *All Their Future* (Penguin Books 1968)
8 B. Allen (ed) *Headship in the 1970s* (Basil Blackwell 1968)
9 *Home and School* (Inner London Education Authority)
10 *Parent/Teacher Relations in Primary Schools, Education Survey No 5* (HMSO 1968)
11 M. Furlong 'The Parent's Role' *Teacher's World* 13th September 1968
12 L. Ridgway and I. Lawton *Family Grouping in the Primary School* (Ward Lock Educational 1965 second edition 1968)
13 M. Young *Innovation and Research in Education* (Routledge and Kegan Paul 1965)
14 M. Young and P. McGeeney *Learning Begins at Home* (Routledge and Kegan Paul 1968)
15 P. McGeeney *Parents Are Welcome* (Longmans 1969) preface by Sir John Newsom
16 R. G. Cave and R. O'Malley *Education for Personal Responsibility* (Ward Lock Educational 1967)

# Chapter 4

# EDUCATION FOR CHANGE

Before discussing some further aspects of home/school relationships at the primary and secondary level, it might be useful to look at some general developments in education. During the past ten years or so at both primary and secondary level a revolution has been taking place in many of our schools, a revolution which in some subjects and forms of organization has been so rapid and so successful that pupils, many parents and indeed younger teachers find it difficult to remember the time when it was not in progress. The central tag or slogan which has become attached to this process of change is 'curriculum development' or, to use a more militant-sounding phrase, 'curriculum reform'. It has been claimed, and I believe with every justification, that this growing concern on the part of both teachers and parents with curriculum reform is the most exciting and promising development in British education since the passing of the 1944 Education Act. The actual genesis of this movement, as with all major educational change, is difficult to pinpoint, especially as curriculum reform is under way in all the developed countries.

On this side of the Atlantic much curriculum reform was initiated by individual enthusiasm and experiment on the part of practising teachers. In 1964 the main strands of development were drawn together and provided with a clearing house and focal point with the formation of the Schools Council for Curriculum and Examinations. The terms of reference of the Schools Council specifically state:

The objects of the Schools Council for the Curriculum and

Examinations are to uphold and interpret the principle that each school should have the fullest possible measure of responsibility for its own work, with its own curriculum and teaching methods based on the needs of its own pupils and evolved by its own staff; and .to seek through co-operative study of common problems to assist all who have individual or joint responsibilities for, or in connection with, the schools' curricula and examinations to coordinate their actions in harmony with this principle.[1]

Despite this declared objective there are many teachers who are extremely doubtful as to the value of the Council and some even appear to regard the curriculum development centres, now being set up by most local education authorities, as cells for the propagation of a system which they claim is totally foreign to us—a plot inspired by the Department of Education and Science to establish a standardized curriculum for the whole country, and yet another indication of the ever increasing encroachment of central authority on the freedom of the teacher. Such fears are not to be lightly dismissed, but my personal view is that the teachers centres for curriculum development, well over 300 at the latest count, are likely to have just the opposite effect to that feared, always providing, of course, that they are well staffed, organized and, perhaps most important of all, firmly committed to local needs.

Curriculum development work is based on the concept that there should be a much closer relationship between teachers and researchers and that they should meet together regularly, both to examine and to initiate curriculum development and reform. The professional associations, especially the National Union of Teachers, which itself plays an important part in providing courses of in-service training, have in general welcomed the suggestion that the assessment and trial of new ideas should be an accepted and integral part of teachers' professional commitments. Few things in education are entirely new; this is as true of aspects of curriculum development as it is of anything else. In my own area, for example, there has been a growing emphasis on making wide provision for in-service training, including full cooperation with societies and associations which perform a valuable function in bringing together teachers and others who have common interests.

Right from the start the Schools Council, after expressing the hope that teachers would meet oftener in groups to discuss curriculum problems, encouraged local education authorities to give every possible assistance—in particular to help provide accommodation, apparatus and secretarial assistance. So far as accommodation is concerned this is usually of a workshop character, combining the facilities of a demonstration laboratory (perhaps for languages, mathematics or science) with that of a practical room for the preparation of materials, and in most cases a lounge and an additional room for lectures and discussions. My own authority, a pilot area in the Nuffield Mathematics Project, established as their first venture a mathematics centre, making use of an old village hall on the site of a primary school. The premises consist of a fairly large room, which is well stocked with a wide variety of equipment and offers opportunities either for group work or personal research in mathematics. Occasionally this room is used for lecture/demonstrations by visiting speakers. One section of the building is used by teachers who wish to construct apparatus or equipment and is well furnished with workbenches and tools. A large collection of mathematical equipment is on permanent display, including a variety of modern teaching machines and similar hardware. The comfortably furnished lounge houses a comprehensive reference library of mathematics books covering all age ranges and also contains the authority's library of programmed textbooks. The lounge is provided mainly for relaxation and informal discussion and there are kitchen facilities for preparing hot drinks and food. A Schools Council Working Paper,[2] in discussing the function of such centres, says:

> The most important is undoubtedly to focus local interest and to give teachers a setting within which new objectives can be discussed and defined and new ideas on content and methods in a variety of subjects can be aired. . . . If teachers are to participate fully in the work of curriculum review they need to be made quickly and expertly familiar with important projects as they develop.

Parents have been welcomed into many centres on a truly remarkable scale; there they are given the valuable opportunity to participate in what their children's schools are attempting to achieve.

The local aspect of development work is strongly stressed here because the eventual and logical purpose of centres is not only discussion and the exchange of ideas but the actual production of relevant and meaningful materials designed especially for use by the teachers and pupils in the areas served by the centres. Local development centres enable teachers to experiment and devise materials which are produced with full knowledge of local conditions, and one can think of a number of subject areas where the help of parents would be invaluable. In some centres, encouraging progress has been made in the production of what are known as learning packages—a selection of materials especially designed to fit in with a modern approach. The packages might contain assignment cards, work sheets, programmed texts, film loops, filmstrips, colour slides, photographs, tapes and so on. Sometimes learning packages are given a decided local bias. Obviously materials produced with the special needs of pupils in Wigan in mind may be, and very often should be, completely different from those produced for pupils living in the fens of East Anglia.

One side effect of the rapid growth of the curriculum development movement is that it has helped teachers, parents and pupils—and as we have seen this partnership is in itself a revolutionary concept—to accustom themselves to the idea of change, not as something to be deplored but as an aspect of modern living which should be accepted with eagerness and confidence. No matter how loudly the traditionalists complain, there can be no return to some temptingly comfortable but largely mythical Shangri-la, where educational objectives are crystal clear and innovation cautious and almost imperceptible. The pace of social, economic and cultural change in the world outside the school is so swift and the growth of new techniques and new knowledge so great that a slow and cautious approach to curriculum reform is no longer appropriate. It should of course be stressed that despite the implications of such publications as the *Black Papers*[3] the protagonists of curriculum reform are not advocating the abandonment of all traditional approaches and established subjects. However it is just as necessary to stress that there is a real need to reexamine thoroughly those traditional subjects and methods which the schools may eventually decide to retain. Certainly, a similar analysis of the underlying essentials and logical structures which is at present leading to much new thinking about the teaching of languages, mathematics and the sciences should also be applied to many other areas of knowledge.

Before going on to mention some specific projects, it might be as well to say a little more about the term 'educational objectives' and to touch upon another term which also has a mid-1960s ring about it. I refer to what has become known as 'educational technology'. Such terms obviously smack of 'pedogese' or 'educanto' as it has sometimes been called,[4] but now that they have become common currency there seems little point in not using them. The Schools Council publication *The First Three Years* stresses:

> The other frontier which is particularly difficult to define is that between 'curriculum development' and 'educational technology'. It would indeed be dangerous to try to do so; those who devise new systems of learning need constantly to have in mind the educational objectives which they are pursuing. In severely practical terms, moreover, the development of a new learning programme may—or should—involve much the same kind of thorough trial in real school conditions of various kinds as the Council insists upon in its curriculum projects.

The increasing emphasis on the necessity to define objectives clearly is a reminder that never before in the history of compulsory education has such a large proportion of the population asked questions which up to now have been mainly the concern of professionals. Questions such as 'What subjects should we teach and what are we trying to achieve?' are no longer confined to professional academic discussion. We have already touched upon the growing public concern about education which has found expression in the formation of such bodies as ACE, the Home and School Council and CAASE.

Although a great many more people are now asking questions, the ensuing discussion is still greatly bedevilled by lack of clarity and definition of terms. Fortunately a more scientific approach to the clarification of terms and planning of educational objectives is now emerging.[5] It would of course be foolish to claim that at this stage in its evolution curriculum development can be considered a scientific movement. Much of the evaluation of new projects, for example, seems to be very like the process which has always taken place in school staffrooms, with forceful personalities and verbally gifted opinion leaders making the pace and having their views accepted. Pragmatic assessment by teachers is certainly of the utmost importance as to date we appear to lack any adequate frames of reference for the objective assessment of progress or the correlation of actual classroom practice with research methods and findings. Still, progress is being made and few forward-looking teachers or parents would reject the thesis that, in curriculum development, objectives and not content are the logical starting points for our thinking. 'Why?' should precede 'What?', 'When?' and 'How?' In other words, our first question is 'What is our objective?', then 'What subject matter is to be used?' and 'What learning experiences or situations are to be provided?' Evaluation is, of course, of great importance and it is in this area that parents are increasingly making themselves heard. Unfortunately, evaluation appears to some extent to have become the battle cry of those who are opposed to curriculum reform in any shape or form—an odd situation when one considers that even in the traditional organization of education, apart from a notoriously unreliable examination system, evaluation is mainly subjective.

Educational technology—as was pointed out above—is an area which overlaps with curriculum development insofar as those who devise and make use of new systems of learning need constantly to ask what objectives they are pursuing. The term educational technology has come to embrace far more than mechanical and electronic devices. In fact it is concerned with the whole new technology of learning and organization—team teaching, heterogeneous groupings, language laboratories, programmed learning, reading laboratories, television and broadcasting, film projectors, light pencils and touch sensitive surfaces, overhead projectors, talking typewriters, computer aided instruction, information retrieval systems and other such innovations. The business firms are right to talk about the necessity of lifting education out of what they plainly regard as an antiquated and inefficient rut, but teachers are also right to point out that there are many questions to be discussed before they wholeheartedly welcome some of the innovations. For example, is it possible to reconcile the large group aspects of team teaching with progressive theories of child-centred education and individual instruction? It may be that individual teaching machines or a school resources centre helps to achieve what is sometimes a desirable one to one relationship, where teacher and taught move forward at the same pace. In working through a programme, a pupil is in a very private sense doing it for himself with all that this means in the educative process. It has been said that each individual has a learning pattern which is as unique as his fingerprints. Technology may help us both to cope with and take advantage of this uniqueness.

As examples of actual curriculum projects now underway in this country, the Schools Council is joint sponsor, with the Nuffield Foundation, of a Resources for Learning Project. The same two organizations have together sponsored development work in mathematics, science and the teaching of French. Another Schools Council project is an investigation of the curriculum needs of children between the ages of eight and thirteen, and there is a major survey in compensatory education with the aim of helping teachers make good the deficiencies which stem from deprivation. Of special interest to the subject of this book, it has been agreed to assist a study of ways in which teachers and parents can best cooperate to help children benefit from their schooling. Other projects already commissioned, or in an advanced state of planning, include one in environmental studies concerned with enhancing children's experience of the world immediately around them.

As Derek Morrell, then Joint Secretary of the Schools Council, pointed out in a talk given in 1966,[6] we must make new educational choices and go on doing so for as long as our condition remains one of change. There is no inconsistency between this and recognizing tradition as one of the sources from which the schools continue to draw strength. It is not tradition itself that change calls in question, but unexamined tradition. A tradition which, when re-examined, appears to be as valid as when it was formulated gains in strength from being consciously revalidated.

One of the aspects of our system which is undergoing rigorous re-examination at the moment—and the one with which this book is mainly concerned—is the importance of parent/teacher cooperation; it is heartening to note that the past year or so has seen a decided quickening of interest in and an appreciation of the vital importance of this cooperation in many quarters. For example, early in 1969 the National Union of Teachers issued a policy press statement, stressing that it has always fully supported the principle of home/school relationships and suggesting some of the ways in which cooperation could best be put into effect.[7] Both the opening sentences and the closing paragraph of the statement emphasized the importance of establishing the correct relationship right from the beginning of compulsory schooling, beginning: 'If the habit of cooperation between home and school is not established at primary school level it can never be fully restored later' and concluding: 'The foundations, like those of education matters generally, must be well laid in the primary school.'

The union's statement adopts a similar stance to Plowden and such publications as Education Survey No 5, when it says that the setting up of a parent teacher association is 'at its most valuable when it makes successful efforts to bring in all parents, and least valuable, in terms of the needs of the child, when it consists of a self-sufficient gathering of like-minded activists often from one social group only'. Once again attention is drawn to the difficulties inherent in the fact that the value orientations and aspirations of middle-class and working-class parents may be poles apart.

The term parent teacher association has been used throughout the preceding chapters, although as Education Survey No 5 makes clear:

There is no uniformity either in the constitution or the

activities of associations which bring parents and teachers together. Some are designated 'parents' associations'; some include past parents; most are for parents and teachers; some are open to all members of the community and virtually become community associations even though they may be known as a 'Friends of the School Association'. Some associations dispense with a subscription so that all parents automatically become members. Many associations have a formal constitution often following the model set out by the National Federation of Parent Teacher Associations; others have 'a loose casual organization' or no constitution at all. All types have been defended by heads on the grounds that they help to safeguard the professional freedom of the schools and allow for adaptation as the needs of school and community change.

For the sake of simplicity I will continue to use the term parent teacher association when describing forms of organizations designed to bring parents and teachers into cooperation.

It is difficult to give any accurate assessment of the strength of parent teacher associations in this country. The National Federation of Parent Teacher Associations, which was founded in 1956, represents an estimated 70,000 parents and teachers, but probably only a small proportion of the countries' associations are affiliated.[8] This may be compared with the 13 million membership of the American National Congress of Parents and Teachers, which was founded in 1897. Holland was even earlier in the field—a national organization was formed in 1866 to further parent/teacher cooperation. In Britain it was not until 1929 that a number of small groups came together to form the first Home and School Council of Great Britain. This body ceased to exist in the early 1950s.

In October 1967 the new Home and School Council was formed, which represented a partnership between the Advisory Centre for Education (a body with headquarters in Cambridge, which gives advice on a variety of educational subjects to its 25,000 members and publishes a periodical 'Where'), the National Federation of Parent Teacher Associations and the Confederation for the Advancement of State Education. This last body developed from a local association which was founded in Cambridge in 1961 and now consists of about 120 local associations, each covering the area of a local education authority. All three of the above organizations will retain their own identity and continue their activities, while the new Home and School Council will 'invite affiliations from schools as well as from parent groups and from individuals and will provide stimulus and advice for schools through a publication supplementary to those already produced and through pamphlets on various facets of home and school relations'. Mention has already been made of the other main voluntary body relevant to our subject, i.e. the Pre-School Playgroups Association, which was begun in 1961.

While most educationists are in favour of more parent/teacher cooperation, the advantages and disadvantages of formal associations have been, and no doubt will continue to be, hotly debated. My own view is that in all but the smallest rural primary schools, formal parent teacher associations, however loosely organized, have a valuable function to perform. That teachers' associations still have some reservations may be seen in the NUT policy statement which stresses:

> It would be quite wrong for discussion and criticism to be allowed on the basis of the comparison of one school with another, one teacher or one class with another, or even one method with another if this involved value judgments as opposed to enlightenment. It is therefore of the utmost importance that limitations of this kind should be clearly understood and that the head and his colleagues should retain overall control and responsibility, whatever kind of organization is set up.

The statement also points out:

> Teachers have traditionally given fully and freely of their private time in the interests of their pupils, and will continue to do so. They rightly resent, however, proposals that seem to take it for granted that their involvement, in one particular way or another, can be assumed. It is therefore necessary to insist that teachers have the same right as

other citizens to decide how they shall spend their own time, freely and without restriction.

Certainly, it is worth remembering that some teachers may really wish to spend extra time in the school but for a variety of reasons cannot. For example, a young female teacher may leave a few minutes after the school closes each day. This anxiety to get away may not be because she is off to enjoy herself but because she has an invalid parent who needs her care. A young male married teacher with a family may miss some evening parent/teacher functions, perhaps because he is engaged in evening institute lecturing or some other form of extra work to augment what is still a fairly low salary. In addition, many teachers of all ages spend a considerable amount of free time in private study, either to improve their professional competence or, understandably, to improve their chances of promotion.

A major gain of improved parent/teacher relationships might be the correction of the often false and outmoded stereotype parents have of teachers and, just as often, teachers of parents. There may well be a few men teachers who fit the old tag 'man among boys but a boy among men' but there are a great many more who do not. The idea of the rather prim spinster school-marm dies hard, but in general, especially with the influx of married women teachers, this is another hopelessly outdated stereotype. Still it is true that some parents never see even one of their child's teachers during the whole of his school life, and when one remembers that their view of teachers (and sometimes the teachers' view of the parents) is based on the child's reports—sometimes exaggerated—and their own childhood memories, one can understand why there are so many misconceptions on both sides.

This mention of exaggerated or false reporting on the part of children brings us to an aspect of parent/teacher relationships which is sometimes very disconcerting. No matter what information teachers may have about parents' personal lives, they are expected to treat such details with the same confidence as one would expect from a priest or a doctor. On the other hand, unfortunately, the slightest tittle-tattle or gossip about a member of a teaching staff seems to be regarded as fair comment by many parents. This is perhaps one of the factors which makes for hesitancy in relationships between parents and teachers. Schools employ enough people to have their fair share of sinners and saints and, what is more to the point, the usual proportion of human beings with ordinary failings and weaknesses. Almost everything a teacher says or does is open to misinterpretation. Young people are skilful at seeing double meanings in innocent remarks and although this is usually humorous it can occasionally become malicious. It is to some extent understandable that teachers are overcautious and sometimes appear to be a little prim in their conversation and behaviour in the presence of both pupils and parents.

That teachers, even young ones at the beginning of their career, can be prejudiced against parents as a body can be illustrated by the comment of one probationer teacher in a junior school, who said: 'Attack the parents first before they attack you.'[9] There is, in fact, some evidence that many teachers are prejudiced in favour of middle-class children; an overcensorious attitude on the part of some teachers towards what they consider to be working-class lack of responsibility also makes for difficult relationships. Attitudes such as these are probably not typical and represent the extremes, but there are ignorant and prejudiced teachers, just as there are ignorant and prejudiced parents.

A much more common and therefore perhaps more serious fault is that many teachers, themselves the product of an improved system of state education, fail to realize that that system has also produced better educated and more enlightened parents. In other words, some teachers, including some young ones for whom there is little excuse, still carry a stereotype of over-anxious or ill-educated parents, which may fit more with their recollection of their own parents than with the parents of the children they teach in the school. So far as over-anxiety is concerned, obviously many parents over-estimate their children's abilities, but this is not a fault unknown in teachers who are also parents; certainly it is one which the intelligent teacher will understand. A sensitive teacher will also understand that a parent may well feel a little jealousy when

77

she ceases to be the centre of her child's world and has to put up with a continuous barrage of 'Miss Jones tells us to do it this way. . . .' It is at the junior stage that such a reaction is most common and it is at this stage that parent/teacher relationships need to be strengthened and firm foundations consolidated. The cutting of the apron strings on the part of the junior child should be welcomed as a forward step in his development, not thought of as a cause for friction between parents and teacher.

In general however the prospect for improved home/school relationships at the junior stage is bright, as we shall discuss in the next chapter.

References

1 Schools Council *The First Three Years: 1964/67* (HMSO 1968)
2 Schools Council *Working Paper No 10: Curriculum Development—Teachers' Groups and Centres* (HMSO 1966)
3 C. B. Cox and A. E. Dyson (eds) *Fight for Education—A Black Paper* and *Black Paper Two* (Critical Quarterly Society 1969)
4 A. Clegg and B. Megson *Children in Distress* (Penguin 1968)
5 B. S. Bloom and others *Taxonomy of Educational Objectives* vols 1 and 2 (Longmans 1956)
6 D. H. Morrell *Education and Change* (College of Preceptors 1966)
7 NUT News Release (14th March 1969)
8 *Parent/Teacher Relations in Primary Schools, Education Survey No 5* (HMSO 1968)
9 M. Collins *Students into Teachers* (Routledge and Kegan Paul 1969)

Chapter 5

# ACTIVITY AND EXPERIENCE

Throughout this book use has been made of the term 'a good progressive approach' and before discussing home/school relationships at the primary stage I will briefly describe what I understand by this term so far as the education of young children is concerned. Although we have already discussed pupils of 5 to 7 years of age I will continue to write about 'the primary school' as much of what is said in this chapter is relevant to the whole of the primary age range. My personal bias is very much towards a progressive and intelligently structured problem-solving and child-centred approach. I believe not only that this is the right direction for education at both primary and secondary stages but also that in this type of school the necessary experiments and developments in parent/ teacher cooperation are most likely to be undertaken. I define a good progressive approach as one where there is little emphasis placed on formal teaching and the amassing of irrelevant factual knowledge. Instead the pupils are encouraged to learn through discovery whenever this is both possible and desirable, and one of the teacher's major educational aims, even with young children, is the development of reflective and critical thinking.

As was stressed in the early chapters it is mainly in our schools for younger children that the progressive approach to education has been most fully developed. We have noted that as long ago as 1931 the Hadow Report on *The Primary School*[1] recommended that: 'The curriculum is to be thought of in terms of activity and experience rather than knowledge to be acquired and facts to be stored.' More than three decades later in the introductory chapter to the Plowden Report, the following questions were asked: 'Has "finding out" proved to be better than "being told"? Has the emphasis which the Hadow Report placed on individual progress been justified by its results? Do children learn more through active co-operation than by passive obedience?' The background research carried out for the Plowden Committee by H.M. Inspectors showed that some five years ago in about a third of our primary schools the above questions could be answered with a categorical affirmative and in another third a rather more qualified agreement. However if progress in my own authority is any guide, I would say that the swing towards progressive child-centred methods, although somewhat modified and refined by the curriculum development movement, has gained rapidly in momentum since this study was carried out. The continuance of this swing is by no means inevitable however; a number of influential people believe it to be undesirable in its present form—a threat to what they plainly regard as established and well-tried values. For example, in the Critical Quarterly Society's *Fight for Education—A Black Paper* and *Black Paper Two* edited by C. B. Cox and A. E. Dyson,[2] some very heated if rather illogical arguments are advanced against 'the revolutionary changes which have taken place in English education since the end of the Second World War'. The papers are introduced by a 'Letter to Members of Parliament' and as early as the first sentence of the first paper there is a reference to what the authors call 'the introduction of free play methods' into primary schools—a description of the modern approach which I have not actually heard used by teachers for more than twenty years. In the letter the authors claim that some primary teachers are taking to an extreme the belief that children must not be told anything but must find out for themselves. The letter goes on: 'Parents, children, students and teachers are to be forced to accept the new changes whether they like them or not.'

The authors appear to believe that the present student unrest has its roots in progressive methods in the primary school

During a workshop session at the Stapleford Mathematics Centre, Cambridgeshire, parents learn about the work their children are doing by doing it themselves. They can also see their children's work, and experiment with the apparatus used in the modern approach to mathematics.

ROBIN KEMPSTER

A mum gives practical help in cookery class. Almost all parents have something to give to the school; they need only be interested and encouraged.

and quote Timothy Raison, who wrote in the *Evening Standard* for 15th October 1968:

> Nevertheless, the art students often embody the innocence, the passionate belief that if you would only leave people alone their best would come out, that is the attractive element in true, non-violent anarchism. . . . And this romantic view is widespread, not merely among art students, but many others who are likely to be marching. . . . I sometimes wonder whether this philosophy—which I am sure many of the protest marchers feel, however inarticulately—does not owe at least something to the revolution in our primary schools. Influenced by a variety of psychologists from Freud to Piaget, as well as by educational pioneers from Froebel onwards, these schools have increasingly swung away from the notion (which characterizes secondary education) that education exists to fit certain sorts of people for certain sorts of jobs, qualifications and economic roles, to the idea that people should develop in their own way at their own pace. Competition has given way to self-expression. And now this has worked its way up to the student generation. They don't want to be chivvied through exams onto a career ladder; they want to be (what they conceive to be) themselves; and if the system stands in the way of this, marching about Vietnam in some indefinable way enables them to make a protest against the system and in favour of something better. At times one can imagine them, like infants' schoolchildren on television singing: 'There is a happy land, far far away.'

My own belief is about as far removed from this view as it is possible to get. If some students blow their top once they reach university, the cause is far more likely, in the majority of cases, to be found in a reaction against the formality and repression of many of our grammar schools rather than in the fact that they have been taught to think for themselves at primary level. It is perhaps significant that in the so-called *Black Paper* the highly critical chapter on 'Freedom in Junior Schools' is in fact written by the headmistress of a grammar school. She states as one of her arguments that 'A child who has always followed her (sic) own inclination finds it hard to sit down and learn his (sic) French and Latin verbs or his tables.'

Obviously there are many dangers if an unthinking progressive approach is applied in a random fashion, and some thought-provoking arguments are put forward in *Perspectives on Plowden*.[3] However as Professor Basil Bernstein points out in that book, 'the once favoured pastime of "waiting for Plowden" has given way to the rapidly institutionalized sport of baiting it.' According to a newspaper report discussing the publication of the first *Black Paper*, the team responsible plan to mount a public campaign to muster support from parents and teachers by holding public meetings and issuing further publications. Even here, as in so many other matters touched upon in this book, we appear to be following the example set by the United States, although in this case some few years later. Now, when American educationists are exhibiting a renewed interest in British progressive methods and rehabilitating their own John Dewey's ideas, our educational conservatives appear to have decided to mount an all-out offensive. Student unrest appears to have sparked off the conservative movement in Britain. In the United States it was when the Russians launched their first Sputnik that a scapegoat was needed to account for the apparent failure of the American system of education. The progressive movement in education was an obvious choice and the traditionalists were marshalled under the leadership of such powerful individuals as Vice-Admiral Hiram Rickover and Dr Max Rafferty, Superintendent of Public Schools in California.

There are obvious dangers in the unintelligent application of pupil-centred permissiveness and in an unwise concentration on learning through discovery. Emotional argument, unsupported by facts, quite rightly does little to sway those teachers and parents who are for clearly defined discipline, authority and a traditional, subject-centred curriculum. A major difficulty facing protagonists of progressive education is that in some areas aims are so wide and so subjective that it is difficult to formulate acceptable evidence that objectives have been achieved. As I have pointed out elsewhere[4] already some of the teachers involved in the various Nuffield projects are faced with a dilemma concerning the evaluation of the results of applying new methods with their pupils—although from their experience they are quite happy to make a value judgment that the new approach is far more valuable than the work they did in the past. Unfortunately, there are at present no easy ways of testing much of what they believe they are accomplishing with their pupils. This does not necessarily mean that little is happening or that useful objectives are not being achieved—merely that our present techniques for measurement are inadequate. As a comparison, imagine a student educated by Cambridge-type new morality theologians sitting an examination in religious knowledge set by a fundamentalist preacher from Tennessee.

Certainly we need a great deal of trial and experiment, and a number of distinguished educationists—Professor P. H. Hirst for example—have advanced very cogent arguments for the view that while some change is both desirable and necessary there are serious weaknesses in both the traditional and progressive approach.[5] The important thing is that there should be constant experiment and rational—not emotional and uninformed—discussion about new methods. It is a caricature to describe our primary schools as places where children do as they please, and conservative-minded academics show a startling ignorance of the facts when they line themselves up with those who complain 'they don't learn them nothing nowadays'. The strength of the modern progressive approach lies in its concern for the individual rather than the class unit: a concern which each new development in psychology and sociology shows as a very necessary approach to education. To many parents and teachers, treating boys and girls as individuals appears to be so self-evident a way of setting about education that it hardly needs stating, yet much of the present backlash against progressive methods in schools is in essence a plea for a return to formal class teaching methods.

How does one know a good progressive primary school? Probably the first thing that one notices upon entering such a school is the purposeful hum of activity and the overt confirmation of the statement 'a school is children'. Corridors, cloakrooms, outside areas—all will be in use as work spaces and the pupils' work will be tastefully displayed in every possible space. The classrooms will not be self-contained units (and indeed in a modern school will not have been built as such) and a variety of work may be going on at the same time in any one room—painting, modelling, scientific and mathematical experiments, dramatic play and so on. Only rarely will every member of the class be engaged in the same activity. Furniture will be arranged informally—although much thought is given to the most suitable arrangement—and where there is a teacher's desk it will not be a focal point. Subject divisions are blurred, the time-table elastic and age groups merged. Carried to its logical conclusion this form of organization becomes an 'integrated day'.[6] Just as many infant heads are finding that the system of family grouping is a useful method of introducing modern infant methods to parents, many junior heads are finding this is true about the integrated day. For example, Mr R. L. Kilsby, Head of Croxton County Primary School, Cambridgeshire and the Isle of Ely, has written the following description of how this form of organization has been adapted for use in a small rural school:

The Integrated Day

1 *Half-term topic or centre of interest* This is a vital part of the system for it means that work is really integrated. It is the central theme for art, projects (both group and individual) and English. It also provides for frequent and necessary occasions when all the juniors are brought together, for discussion, to view one another's work and to listen to talks on the theme, either by themselves, the teacher or, where possible, visiting speakers. Every effort is made to arrange an educational visit relating to the topic and this is made possible by generous financial help from the parents. Previous topics have included transport, Canada and the zoo, and the current theme is housing.

2 *Daily number work* Each child is expected to do some number work each day, although in practice this means that all except the youngest children must do a satisfactory amount each week. During the past term almost every

child has asked to do some part of his mathematics at home.

3 *English work*   Although the central theme gives rise to a great deal of English work, weekly or fortnightly assignments are also set. In addition each child has a diary and a workbook, although the use a child makes of these varies considerably from individual to individual. All marking is done in the presence of the child and any necessary practice is given informally when the need arises.

4 *Art*   This includes needlework. Assignments are given which may or may not be related to the central theme. The big room is divided into library, mathematics and art areas and it will be appreciated that the problems which can be posed by 30 children working with papier mâché or clay are much reduced when the groups consist of no more than three or four working on any activity at one time.

5 *Television lessons*   Extensive use is made of television lessons and they are supervised by the part-time teacher, whose own timetable is largely determined by transmission time. They fit admirably into the integrated day since the group watching any programme moves into the television room at the appropriate time and the teacher is free to make as much or as little use of the programme as she considers necessary. Some programmes may instigate work which is open-ended, with groups or individuals following lines of enquiry for some time; others may merely need a brief summing up.

6 *Workcards*   Use is made of commercially produced assignment cards, such as the Ladybird workcards, science workcards, and the Hulton workcards. Each card may be an end in itself or the starting point for further work.

*Records*
Each child fills in his or her own timetable on a duplicated form, each form covering a fortnight's work. These timetables were especially useful in the early days of this form of organization since block graphs were drawn which showed how much time each child was spending on individual subjects. The teacher keeps a record of the

work done by each child, together with other aspects such as significant social behaviour. It is hoped in time to produce a suitable file on each child but so far the most convenient form for such a file has not been found.

*Conclusions*

It is far too early for any firm conclusions to be drawn but the results are sufficiently encouraging for us to persevere. One important benefit is that the children appear to be happy (an increasing number decline the opportunity for their traditional playtime) and this is invaluable in helping to establish parent cooperation. There would also appear to be an improvement in reading resulting from increased motivation and the individual approach. Certainly the amount of reading, both in search of factual knowledge and for pleasure, has considerably increased. It can also be said that behaviour problems are less apparent and that the traditional nuisance, the child who cannot sit still or stop talking, has his nuisance value much reduced in the atmosphere of the integrated classroom. To operate the integrated day calls not only for hard work but for a fundamental change in attitude both towards school and towards the way in which children learn. I have been most fortunate in having an enthusiastic staff and co-operative parents who have approached this experiment with open minds.

An educational approach based on learning through discovery can be justified if, and only if, the teacher plays a full part and is fully aware of what this part needs to be. The onus is upon the teacher to structure a learning environment, and a problem-solving education needs to be constantly examined in the light of both the needs of the child and the broader demands made upon the education system by society. The needs of the moment must also be balanced with those expected to exist in the future. To allow a child to explore and discover freely is certainly of central importance, although as Professor Richard Peters has pointed out, children's curiosity is sporadic and differs greatly from child to child so that what must be developed is a 'disciplined curiosity'.

A visitor going into a traditional school may find the exact opposite to the situation described above. The school is almost certain to have an unnatural, monastic quiet about it, with no sign of children outside the classrooms except for the occasional child who is on his way to the cloakroom or has been sent on a 'message'. Little or no children's work will be displayed on the walls which, as often as not, are bare except for the odd repro- duction of 'When Did You Last See Your Father?' or 'The Boyhood of Raleigh', together with honours boards, school rules, fire regulations and so on. The classes will probably be streamed by ability, the desks stand in serried ranks and the majority of books in the classrooms will be formal textbooks. Teachers will spend much time seated at their desks, often with long lines of children waiting for their exercise books to be marked, not with constructive comment but with ticks or so many out of ten. Parents visiting schools such as these may find little change in methods or organization since their own school- days—in fact, little evidence of change since the pupils' grand- parents were at school. Few parents who remember such schools from their own younger days will be very impressed by the arguments put forward by the authors of such publications as the *Black Papers*. To take just one aspect, the traditional class teaching situation to which the educational conservatives would wish us to return is very much geared towards the middle child. Both the slow-learning and the gifted child suffer in such schools. The personal needs of the deprived, handicapped or disturbed child are very likely to be overlooked completely.[7] One note of warning should however be sounded: Perhaps even in the most progressive primary schools the exceptionally gifted child, especially one with artistic gifts, may not get the attention he needs, although little can be done about this on a large scale until there are more special schools such as the Royal Ballet School and the Yehudi Menuhin School.

This present book is not the place to describe in any detail the changes and developments which have taken place in primary education during the past decade or so, but it might be relevant to touch upon some of the topics which usually arise when teachers and parents of children of junior school age meet. Even in an age when education is making increasing use of the hardware of technology, and materials grouped together into learning packages are making their appearance, books are still the very heart of our educational system. Many primary schools are proud of their central library but my own strong preference is that at the primary stage as many books as possible should be housed in the classroom, leaving only a small, central reference section of books which are either very expensive or not possible or desirable to duplicate. Many experienced teachers would not share my views on this subject, but on more than one occasion I have stood in a school library and listened to its usefulness described in glowing terms, while noting that during the sometimes very lengthy discussions that have ensued, not a single child has entered the room. If a primary school is lucky enough to have an extra room designated as a library it might do well to follow the example of some of the schools who have turned this room, often with parental help, into a learning resources centre, which is a long way removed from the all too common nineteenth-century type reading room.

A distinguished educationist stated recently that there were too many books being published in this country, and one can see something of the reasoning behind this statement if one's attention is drawn, as mine is almost every day through the post, to the ever increasing output of the publishing houses. A busy teacher or a concerned parent has to make his choice from a bewildering selection, all claiming to be the most up-to-date work on the subject concerned. Some schools have experimented with regular book exhibitions and such exhibitions are most valuable in allowing parents and teachers to examine books at their leisure and play a most useful part in ensuring that they are able to make the best possible selection. If I may use yet another example from my own authority, the part played by parents in such an exhibition is described by Mr G. Hamilton, Headmaster of Haslingfield Endowed School, Cambridgeshire and Isle of Ely, in the following note, which is reproduced in full as it is of obvious relevance:

The parent teacher association has recently been reconstituted to admit members who are not parents of children at the school. The main object of this was to attract parents of pre-school children, but older people have also joined, making it in effect a village association based on the school. Obviously our main links with our children's homes are through this association, which sponsors a wide range of activities. Through the PTA we organize discussion groups, which meet fortnightly, with an attendance of about 12 and a total membership of about 30. These groups occasionally widen out as special topics are followed and lead to such things as meetings with LEA officials to discuss secondary reorganization. Larger numbers attend for visits from specialist speakers. These activities are designed to cover the educational side of the association. Social functions include film weekends—Friday for parents, Saturday morning for children—a Christmas Party and a Drama Group.

I make a point of visiting parents and talking to them in their homes—this is much easier to do in a village—and inviting them to join activities which suit them. This has resulted in some of the more diffident parents helping in various ways, such as making scenery for the stage, making apparatus for school use, and helping with the swimming pool—cleaning and repairing. Other parents come into school during the day to sew curtains, repair and cover books, help with swimming, netball or country dancing, and, most important, talk to the children. Parents are engaged in outside activities with the children. One mother runs a toy-making class on Saturday mornings in the winter; others have groups of boys and girls in their homes making sweets and cakes. The parents have a rota for looking after the swimming pool during the holidays and fathers come in to help beginners learn to swim.

Perhaps the most important of these activities is the book exhibition which has become firmly established as an annual event. It was begun to interest parents in their children's reading and certainly aroused a lot of interest in children's books in general. This year well over 1,000 books were on display, taken from the shelves of Cambridge bookshops, together with added attractions in the shape of models and toys. The parents have a rota for looking after the exhibition, which is open for six hours each day, as well as constructing bookstands and erecting and dismantling the exhibits. This year the staff and I presented an eight-week course on modern mathematics, which was well attended, and a repeat has been requested. Next year we hope to have a series to advise parents on how best to help their children, run by the staff and, we hope, experts from the authority. We have found after operating an 'open school' policy that it is not enough simply to tell parents they are welcome. Ways must be found of attracting their interest. We are really only at the beginning and a lot remains to be done before we are satisfied that the children are reaping the full benefit of their parents' participation.

Mr Hamilton is very much alive to the fact that concrete and practical help can be given in the field of reading. The Plowden survey showed that two-thirds of unskilled workers had five books or fewer in the home, apart from children's books or magazines; a twentieth of the professional workers had fewer than five books. Perhaps the last part of this statement is more surprising than the first, although Richard Mabey has pointed out in his introduction to the book *Class*,[8]

> The common assumption about the 'bookishness' of the middle-class home, however, is probably based on a myth. The library in such a home consists more often than not of para-books, like the Reader's Digest condensations, which can hardly claim to be of more educational value than the few prison-camp escape stories that may make up the working-class family's collection.

Many working-class parents would welcome guidance about the use of libraries, both with regard to their own reading and the choice of reading material for their children. Often they are unaware that public libraries usually have a section which caters especially for younger readers. Parents' knowledge of books is often limited to comic annuals or sets of expensive encyclopedias bought on hire purchase after a hard sell by some door-to-door salesman.

The whole subject of reading is one which appears to arouse a high degree of emotional involvement on the part of parents. Perhaps this is because they believe that reading is the one skill in which they are capable of measuring achievement; certainly in the early days of schooling it is mainly upon the child's reading performance that the parents base their judgment of the efficiency of the school. As many teachers of infants know, to their cost, it is difficult to convince parents that there needs to be a time of socialization and language experience before real reading can begin. So much publicity is given to the children who fail to make progress in reading that it is often forgotten how successful most teachers are in bringing the majority of children to the stage where they read skilfully, both for pleasure and for understanding. Fortunately there are few teachers who still believe that 'barking at print' and 'reading with understanding' are the same process, although a number of parents seem to be quite happy once the barking at print stage has been reached. Reading is essentially a means of communication and it is not enough to make the appropriate noises in response to printed symbols on a page. This is not to deny or minimize the importance of the fact that the child has to make the appropriate noises before he can read with meaning. Obviously certain mechanical skills are necessary but the mere achievement of these skills does not in itself ensure real success. The problem for the teacher is to strike the right balance between 'recognition teaching' and 'teaching for content'. Perhaps the over-anxious parent can be excused when one considers the variety of methods of teaching reading in use, which in themselves are a continuing source of controversy within the profession. There is still no general agreement on the relative merits of 'phonic' methods on the one hand and 'look and say' on the other. Some teachers believe explicitly in the sentence approach and others are passionate advocates of such new schemes as the initial teaching alphabet or words in colour. As there is no single method generally accepted it is perhaps to be expected that the press and other mass media give the teaching of this subject a great deal of publicity, often uninformed. The parents may well be left with the impression that one method is used to the total exclusion of all others and that this is responsible for success or failure. To anyone who has the slightest acquaintance with the teaching of reading in our schools this is clearly nonsense. Every good infant teacher knows that at some stage the 'sounds' of letters have to be learnt by young children. The controversy arises with regard to the questions when and how.

For full parent/teacher cooperation in the teaching of reading it is necessary to undertake a great deal of 'parent education' especially to explain the vital importance of vocabulary growth and concept formation through pre-reading experiences. In practice this may prove to be a difficult task indeed. Whereas it is fairly easy in explaining the new approach in mathematics to devise situations where the average parent is as unsophisticated a subject as his son or daughter, it is rather more difficult for parents to think themselves back to the stage when their own vocabulary about everyday things was as limited as their children's.

A great deal of new apparatus and equipment has been marketed recently. Of the many new reading schemes the one which has had the most publicity is Pitman's initial teaching alphabet, originally known as the augmented roman alphabet. It is in fact so well known that a detailed description is unnecessary and many parents will know that ita is the normal alphabet with two letters dropped and twenty other symbols added to represent additional sounds. It is still too early to say whether ita lives up to all the claims which have been made for it, but certainly it appears to be partly responsible for the growing interest in the teaching of reading. A few years ago it would have been difficult to predict how increasing mechanization in the classroom could have any bearing on the teaching of this subject. There are however one or two indications that in reading, as in most other subjects, modern educational technology may have a part to play. For example, teachers are experimenting with adapted filmstrip projectors as an improvement on the flash-card technique, and a number of machines have been marketed recently for correcting faulty eye movements and improving reading speed. There are also some very expensive machines, such as the talking typewriter, on the market and it seems probable that smaller machines may soon be available at more conservative prices. Expensive hardware may belong to the school of the future, but many schools are now making use of the 'language master'. This machine is about the size of a portable tape recorder and my own experience leads me to the conclusion that it is a most significant contribution to the teaching of reading—especially as it costs only as much as a medium-priced recorder.

Another new approach being tried in many schools is the reading laboratory, a rather grand name for what is really a carefully graded selection of comprehension material. These laboratories were developed in America, although there is now a British reading workshop on the market,[9] and are intended to improve such aspects of reading as comprehension and speed. During recent years a number of experiments have been carried out with laboratories to test their effectiveness. Judged by results it would appear that teachers still have much to learn about what can be achieved by the introduction of carefully graded reading materials. Whether these materials are in the form of a laboratory or the more familiar textbook does not seem to be the most important factor; provided carefully graded material is used for regular daily sessions, one can expect significant improvement in reading and comprehension performance. One advantage of the laboratory cards and workbooks, like that of the new mathematics workshop cards, is that they are self-correcting and carefully graded; thus the teacher does not have to spend time selecting and grading materials, making cards and checking answers.

Much has already been done in educating parents in the methods by which they can help their children tackle the difficult task of reading in the beginning stages. However, much remains to be done. In the United States it has been recognized for many years that reading is a skill which needs to be practised throughout schooling, even at university level. Parents can help right through their children's education by placing emphasis on such skills as finding information and extracting relevant facts, by teaching them to skim—still frowned upon by many teachers but an ever increasing need in our modern world—and by encouraging them to increase their speed and develop the growth of critical powers. Parents

would do well to put their strength behind the present movement to give reading studies the same status in this country as
they have achieved in the United States and encourage their
children to abandon the belief that the teaching of reading
stops at the end of the primary stage. Certainly it is vital that
parents and teachers cooperate to help achieve mastery in this
all-important basic skill.

## References

1  *The Primary School* (HMSO 1931)
2  C. B. Cox and A. E. Dyson (eds) *Fight for Education — A Black
   Paper* and *Black Paper Two* (Critical Quarterly Society 1969)
3  R. S. Peters (ed) *Perspectives on Plowden* (Routledge and Kegan
   Paul 1969)
4  R. G. Cave *All Their Future* (Penguin 1968)
5  J. F. Kerr (ed) *Changing the Curriculum* (University of London
   Press 1968)
6  M. Brown and N. Precious *The Integrated Day in the Primary
   School* (Ward Lock Educational 1968)
7  A. Clegg and B. Megson *Children in Distress* (Penguin 1968)
8  R. Mabey (ed) *Class* (Anthony Blond 1967)
9  *Reading Workshop* (Ward Lock Educational 1969)

Chapter 6

# SOME NEW DEVELOPMENTS

If it is true that reading is the basic subject about which parents feel most competent to help, the exact opposite, certainly so far as most working-class parents are concerned, holds with mathematics. Methods and content have changed so rapidly that many parents, even of the youngest children, feel confused and helpless when asked by their children for help. Up to the beginning of the Second World War, experiment in the teaching of mathematics was in the main confined to the upper age ranges in the grammar school. The first ten post-war years brought some interesting and exciting developments in secondary modern schools, but it was not until the early 1950s that this modern approach made any real impact on the majority of primary schools. Prior to this, the teaching of mathematics to children under the age of 11 was usually thought of as a fairly straightforward process. All too often the aim was to groom children until they achieved a reasonable performance in computation; the serious work in mathematics was left to the secondary school. Discussion in primary school staffrooms, and indeed at parent/teacher meetings, was often limited to such topics as whether tables should be learnt by rote, where to put the '1' or whether it was immoral to teach children to borrow.

In 1953 Miss L. D. Adams, HMI, published *A Background to Primary School Mathematics*. This was followed in 1956 by the Mathematical Association's major report on 'Mathematics in the Primary School'. About the same time reformers such as Dr C. Gattegno and Professor Z. P. Dienes were introducing teachers, and very often parents as well, to the advantages of what are known as 'structural materials' in the teaching of mathematics to young children. Although most teachers worked hard to widen their understanding of the new methods, so many experiments were taking place and conflicting claims being made that it was difficult for the ordinary teacher, let alone a parent, to keep abreast of developments. Discussion at teachers' courses and conferences showed that at both a national and local level, consolidated effort was needed if the revolution in the teaching of mathematics to primary school children was to succeed. This need gave rise to the Nuffield Primary Mathematics Project.

It has long been recognized that it is in the primary school that children's attitudes towards mathematics are formed. Although it is far too early to describe the new approach to mathematics as an unqualified success, certainly experience in the schools encourages one to believe that we are at last moving away from the situation where this is a subject which is disliked, and in some cases feared, by the majority of both teachers and pupils. No doubt the balance which needs to be kept between mathematical problem solving and learning by discovery, and the need in this subject to learn a number of basic facts, will be debated for a long time. The child will certainly appreciate and retain the knowledge that he arrives at through his own efforts—provided of course the teacher makes possible the repeated application of this knowledge. For example, a pupil may learn a mathematical fact by trial and error but unless he is able to apply this knowledge in a variety of problem solving situations it is more than likely he will forget it. Although there must be, in the words of Bertrand Russell, 'An awakening of the learner's belief in reason and his confidence in the truth of what is being demonstrated,' as Professor Peters has pointed out, it would be folly to neglect the importance of practice and precision in extolling the virtues of self-origination. This would appear to be particularly true in regard to mathematics for, as children advance through the primary school, it seems probable that more abstract concepts are formed in this subject than in others.

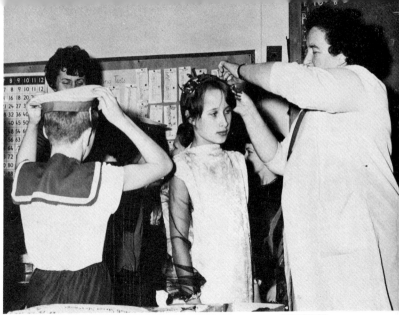

RICHARD DYKES

Mothers help pupils with their costumes for the school play. Special events such as this offer many opportunities for home/school cooperation.

The puppet theatre was made for the school by parents.

HENRY GRANT

School staff can be overwhelmed with paperwork, and parents can help to ease the burden. Here two mothers have volunteered to help with duplicating.

Without the continual exercise of these conceptual schemes they will soon be forgotten. At the later junior and secondary level the number of real life situations with a significant mathematical and practical content become less. This is indeed one of the restricting aspects in applying the principle of learning through discovery to mathematics since so many abstractions occur in this subject. What appears most likely to be gained from learning through discovery in mathematics is a basic understanding of the general strategies of problem solving, as opposed to a particular strategy for solving a particular problem. There would appear to be a question here of immediate aims as opposed to long-term aims. Perception of form, manipulation, exploration and discovery are imperative to a basic understanding of mathematics, but mastery will come only with repeated and precise application of concepts acquired in this way. This in no way need conflict with a progressive approach, as John Dewey wrote: 'Inferences can only occur in a mind that possesses information as to matters of fact but there is all the difference in the world as to whether the acquisition of information is treated as an end in itself or is made an integral part of the training of thought.'[1] In mathematics, along with the continued extension of ideas and techniques, time has to be given to learning basic number facts and whether this becomes wearisome depends mostly on the teacher. The object is to keep a balance between the two apparently opposing ideas that children must sometimes spend time learning facts that are not intrinsically interesting and, on the other hand, that children learn more quickly and lastingly if they are interested.

The questions that need to be constantly asked by parents and teachers are posed in the Schools Council Field Report No 1[2]: 'Can we really be sure that one is doing more than substituting one fashion in mathematics teaching for another?' and 'Are the new ways really better than the old?' Personally I believe that although most teachers are wisely proceeding with some caution, the mere existence of modern mathematics projects has had a most beneficial effect on both primary and secondary schools. The greatest single change is, without doubt, the new enthusiasm aroused for this subject in teachers and children, which may be contrasted to the boredom and sometimes active dislike all too common in the past.

In a previous chapter I have discussed the setting up of curriculum development centres and mentioned the fact that my own authority has established a successful mathematics centre in the village of Stapleford. Much of the work of this centre has been directed towards acquainting parents with the changes that have taken place in modern mathematics and the warden, Mr Tom Christie, has written the following report on this aspect of development work:

It was generally agreed from the outset that an important part of the function of the Stapleford Mathematics Centre would be to keep parents informed as to the purpose and nature of the changes in the curriculum which were taking place in this subject. To do so contact has to be established between the centre and parents living in a widely scattered rural area. It was decided to tackle the problem in three ways: First to make available visiting speakers familiar with the work of the centre to any school parent teacher association where the head was contemplating changes in the traditional syllabus; second, that these speakers should close their talk with a formal invitation to the parents to visit the centre where they could view examples of children's work, see the display of apparatus and, most important of all, try out for themselves the new approach in a workshop session. Last, to get children into the centre from as many schools as possible and then to invite the parents, through their children, to visit the centre and view the work left behind as the result of the children's working sessions. Fortunately, all three approaches aroused considerable interest in parents so that a fourth factor emerged which had not been planned but which resulted in bringing more parents into the centre—it appeared that parents who had visited the centre spoke to many who had not and soon approaches were made by groups of parents from areas where no PTAS existed. This resulted in several new PTAS owing their inception to a workshop visit to the centre by a group of interested parents. When parents visit the centre the group is limited to 24 members— if more wish to come then extra evenings have to be booked to accommodate all without any groups exceeding 24 in number. This restriction allows for plenty of room for movement in the workshop session, and it ensures that any difficulties arising out of the assignment can be dealt with individually. Groups usually arrive at 8.0 p.m., as this is the most convenient time for most parents, particularly those who have young children to put to bed, baby-sitters to arrange for and perhaps anything up to 20 miles to travel to the centre. The atmosphere of the lounge where the groups assemble does much to dispel the understandable feeling of tension and nervousness which most parents appear to experience at the prospect of 'going back to school'. As briefly as possible the purpose and work of the centre is explained in the comfort of the lounge. The group is then invited to spend the next ten minutes in the workroom viewing the display of apparatus and children's work which is a permanent feature of the centre. Although asked specifically not to worry about the assignments and materials spread out on the work-tables, few parents can resist having a nervous look at the workcards which they know they are going to be asked to complete. At this stage they require constant reassuring; many appear to think that their work is going to be marked out of ten and some caustic remark scribbled across it. The workcards themselves are specially written with parents in mind and attempt to show a quick progression from infant to upper junior level on what to most will be a new topic, coupled with a new approach. As it is intended that parents will work in pairs, twelve sets of assignment cards are available on the table, together with the apparatus, paper etc required to complete the assignment. The parents are allowed time for a good look round, then asked to sit down at any table beside the person they intend to work with. Amid protests that they will never be able to do this or that, or that they were never any good at school, they are invited to carry on and shout for help when necessary. The first card being at infant level there is no danger of anyone getting off to anything but a good start and the atmosphere soon changes to one of relief. When teachers are present in the group they simply take a place at any table and work alongside the parent, being careful not to be too clever. Most groups work enthusiastically for the next two hours, refusing a suggested coffee break at about 9.15 p.m. By this time they appear to have got the bit between their teeth and there is no stopping them. Without exception they are most appreciative of the opportunity to have difficulties or misunderstandings, and even prejudices, dealt with individually as they arise. It is not an exaggeration to say that at times it is difficult to get them to go home, and the number of letters from parents that arrive at the centre show how much they appreciate the opportunity of bringing themselves up to date.

Contact is established with parents, through their children, by an activity known as an 'Olympiad'. This is probably a misleading word for, as is made quite clear from the start, there is nothing competitive about this activity. Letters are sent from the centre to numbers of heads inviting them to bring a group of children to the centre during a specified week of term when they will be allocated exclusive use of the centre on any morning or afternoon of their choice. Heads are assured that all that will be expected of their pupils is that each leaves behind some evidence of the fact that he or she has been to the centre and that name and age, but not school, be written on this piece of work. The Olympiad terminates on a Saturday morning when all the children's work which has been accumulated during the week is put on exhibition between 10.0 a.m. and 12.0 noon. Parents whose children are taking part in the Olympiad will already have received, via their children, a printed card inviting them to view this display. The response to this activity has been quite remarkable. As many as 250 parents and children have passed through the centre on a single Saturday morning session at a time when one might have expected traditional Saturday morning activities to have taken preference.

From the experience of this centre one must conclude that given the opportunity (and they should be) parents are intensely interested in current trends in education.

Another example of a new primary subject about which most parents will know very little is physical science. This is a subject which has gained rapid acceptance. As recently as 1959, in an official HMSO publication *Primary Education*,[3] science was dealt with in two pages whereas about twelve were allotted to handwriting. The position is of course different today when almost all primary schools are tackling science in one form or another. A certain amount of physical science has always been taught in good primary schools but it is only within the last few years that this subject has gained general acceptance. When the inclusion of science in the primary school curriculum was first being discussed, some ten years ago, many teachers expressed fears that it would take the place of nature study. This has not happened in most of the schools with which I am acquainted. Nature study has retained its rightful place. It would have been wrong if, in our anxiety to introduce children to science while they are still at the age of wonder, we had left no time for such important activities as exploring the fascinating world that lies beneath the surface of a pond or watching the rooks build at nesting time. One of the most interesting developments is that science in the primary school appears to have had an impact on the teaching of this subject at the secondary stage, especially in the lower forms. It may well be that the lively approach characteristic of the teaching of science in the primary school will eventually alter our methods at the secondary stage which, in the past, often bore little relation to the child's real needs and interests.

Most educationists now appear to be in agreement that science teaching at the primary level should be mainly concerned with the developing of an enquiring attitude of mind rather than the learning of facts. The findings of psychologists such as Piaget[4] suggest that the primary stage is too early to attempt the teaching of scientific laws which, in the event, will probably be only half understood. As more and more primary schools have included the teaching of this subject in their curriculum, teachers have adopted a policy of encouraging the children to devise their own experiments and make their own apparatus. In some schools parents have been most helpful in devising and constructing apparatus and experiments, and in helping children work through experiments in the home, making use of such simple equipment as jam jars, straws, magnets and so on, and many are the reports of both father and children, and often mother too, working deep into the night.

Just as the claim made for physical science to be included in the curriculum was examined carefully before this subject found a place in most primary schools, so the suggestion that a second language should be taught is being considered with similar caution. There are obvious difficulties. In my own authority, a rural area, it is not always possible to ensure that all contributory schools to a particular secondary school teach a second language for at least two years. Most parents welcome the inclusion of a second language, as in the past this was one of the sharp distinctions apparent between those who could afford private education and those whose children attended local authority primary schools. A number of schools have found that in the teaching of a second language by the direct method, the ancillary help of parents has proved of immense value.

Space does not permit a more detailed examination of the primary school curriculum, but the freedom of modern teaching methods and the abandonment of rigid time-tabling has led to more stimulating links between drama, music, art, craft and needlework and the basic subjects. Drama is now recognized as an essential part of the creative life of the child and is receiving much more attention than it has had in the past. Primary schools are encouraged to give music a prominent place in the curriculum and during the past fifteen years broadcast programmes have offered an invaluable contribution in this subject, especially in small rural schools. Many more children now enjoy making music with such

instruments as chime bars and dulcimers. In the early years
of teaching such crafts as needlework the aim is to develop
imagination at an uninhibited and enquiring age. To achieve
this, experiment with materials of all kinds in a way which will
encourage progress and general learning is vital. The initial
stage, properly guided, leads on to project work and in turn
to the emergence of special subjects such as needlework.
In physical education many new developments are taking
place, the emphasis on swimming for example. My colleague,
Mr John Milne, Organizer for Physical Education, Cambridgeshire and the Isle of Ely, has been kind enough to supply
the following note dealing with the impact this new emphasis
on swimming has made on home/school relationships:

Parents are sometimes anxious, through their natural
interest in the academic development of their children, to
take a closer look at the school but unfortunately they are
not always given guidance as to how they can become
partners in the education of their children. Physical
education is an aspect of the curriculum which attracts
those who are anxious to see developed in their children
reasonable skill and good social habits through such
activities as movement, games and dance. Talks and
demonstration lessons on modern methods of physical
education have done much to create an understanding
between the home and the school. However, the greatest
success in this field by this authority has been achieved in
the effort to teach all primary children to swim before
leaving the school. No child can swim without adequate
facilities and since these were limited to occasional periods
at public baths for only a few classes, it was agreed that
extra provision should be made. For obvious financial
reasons expensive concrete pools could not be considered
for every school but, as an experiment, a cheaper sectional
surface pool was purchased for one school and erected
by the parents. This experiment proved to be an unqualified success and has led to a scheme of 50% grant aid
by the authority to any body of parents wishing to have
such a facility at their school. During the past eight years

over 70 pools have been provided on this basis and erected by parents throughout the county, and this is surely testimony to the interest and enthusiasm which could be raised if the school gives a lead. Apart from the rapid progress which has been made in teaching children to swim, of equal concern has been the partnership between parents and the school. The whole venture has involved fund raising committees and working parties of fathers to erect and site the pool, and has developed a team spirit which has surely been of immeasurable benefit to parents and teachers and the whole education service which the authority strives to provide.

Infants have swimming lessons during which mothers are happy to attend to help dress and undress their young children. So it follows that they will have frequent glimpses inside the classroom and regular conversation with the teachers. Swimming clubs have been formed which are organized and supervised by parents out of school hours and during the holidays so there is constant contact between both parties interested in educating young children. This provision in which parents have actively participated has, therefore, been a means of attracting adults to associate themselves directly with the school and, despite themselves perhaps, to take an interest in many other aspects of school life in which previously they might never have believed possible.

Finally, as touched upon in the chapter on curriculum development, the increasing use being made of audio/visual aids in the school reflects the important part that the mass media of communication such as the cinema, radio and television play in everyday life. We live in an age when the mass media, especially television, make a definite impact on all of us, young and old alike. This is possibly more true of pupils of primary school age than any other section of the population.[5] As has often been pointed out, a primary child spends only six and a half hours a day, five out of seven days a week, in the school; the rest of the time in the home environment. Much of this time is spent with the mass media—comics, magazines, radio and especially television. To a very large extent the pattern of media consumption set by the home will determine the child's interests and critical approach to the media. Here then is an important source of both information and entertainment with a decided impact on tastes and attitudes—an area where teacher and parent can work together. In fact, if we accept that television is one of the most important educative—some would say the most educative—agencies in our society, it is an area where teacher and parents *must* work together. At the primary stage the parents not only have control of most of their child's media consumption, but also the responsibility of setting an example so far as a critical and discriminating approach to the media is concerned. It is now considered to be part of the function of a great many schools to undertake media studies and, in fact, actively encourage the development of what might be termed 'consumer resistance'; the weapons in the armoury of the persuaders, be they political or commercial, grow ever stronger,[6] and I have already postulated that one of our main aims in education should be the development of reflective and critical thinking. If both parents and teachers accept this as a common aim then certainly such activities as a child's leisure-time viewing offer fertile ground for encouraging a good educational approach.

Television viewing, as I know from personal experience, is a good starting point for any parent teacher meeting. In television viewing teachers and parents share with children, to some extent, a common experience—one which the adults should seek to capitalize on. It is important however to remember that the child will structure in his own individual fashion what he sees. This basic fact about human psychology makes for great difficulty in predicting the effect of viewing on any particular individual. For example, a great many parents encourage young children to watch certain programmes which they consider to be 'educational' in content—such as some of the travel films shown on children's television and in the early evening programmes, which deal with the exploration of areas where there are rapidly vanishing pockets of uncivilized people. While it is understandable that programme producers should rely heavily on the unusual and the picturesque, it may well be that too many films of this type do much to reinforce in the pupils' minds out-dated and false concepts. This may be partly responsible for the complaint made in *Primary Education* that 'A surprising number of children appear to have the impression that all dwellers in the equatorial forests are pygmies, that Eskimoes live only in igloos and that the western states of America are still ravaged by wars of cowboys and Red Indians.' Some years ago I engaged in some research[7] which strengthened my own belief that the mass media of communication, especially television, played an important part in the propagation of national images. If it is true that young people form many of their stereotypes from viewing, this is of great importance for the teacher and parent, especially with regard to the question of ethnic attitudes. It seems to be the case that even personal experience all too often has little effect on long-standing ethnic attitudes. If we get stuck at the primary level with a picture of the African as a lion-hunting warrior it may well stay with us for a very long time. Geography is sometimes said to be about 'chaps' not 'maps'—this should certainly be remembered by both parents and teachers, who share the important responsibility of ensuring that the child's ideas about 'chaps' of other lands are as up to date and as accurate as possible.

Many parents express concern about the amount of violence depicted on television and often feel guilty that they do not exercise as much censorship as they feel they should. It is admittedly difficult, through research findings, to establish a direct cause and effect relationship between aggressive behaviour in children and violence exhibited on the television screen.[8] In my view there is no doubt that such a relationship exists if only in strengthening existing tendencies to aggression and serving as a model for violent action. A vigorous exponent of the view that much of what is shown on television is harmful to the child is Dr F. W. Wertham, a well-known American psychiatrist, who for many years has conducted an all-out campaign against violence and other undesirable features of the mass media. His influence has been great and there is no doubt that his writings helped towards the alteration of the law on the importation of horror comics into this country.[9]

Most professional psychiatric opinion appears to incline to the view that the mass media in themselves do not create new fears but for certain children precipitate anxieties lying beneath the surface ready to be awakened. It is the phrase 'certain children' that presents the difficulty. Perhaps it is unlikely that the normal well-adjusted child will be warped by occasional exposure to make-believe violence but even if television violence only contributes to basic personality difficulties in a few children, we have no means of protecting those few. It has been pointed out that the insecure or maladjusted child does not wear a label to warn of this condition.

In discussing this subject with mixed audiences of parents and teachers I have found there is genuine concern and the question is often asked 'What can we do?' They might be forgiven for feeling there was indeed little they could do. Most of the protests by educationists, teachers' unions and other organizations concerned have been almost completely ignored, as anyone who remembers the recommendations of the Pilkington Committee[10] will recall. It would seem that the only argument the television companies are prepared to listen to is that presented by audience rating figures. Here then is a valuable field for parent/teacher cooperation. Parents and teachers together can decide whether the duty of the mass media is merely to entertain or also to educate. Switching the programme off is the final deterrent to be used against the producers of undesirable programmes. Perhaps when the parents of this country are better organized we will see more direct action. If, as a result of parents and teachers working together, young people, when adult, demand higher standards in the mass media then we shall have made one of those gains referred to in the Department of Education and Science's Working Paper No 2: 'Which will make it easier for future parents, teachers and others to secure ever larger gains in the education of successive generations of children.'[11]

References

1  J. Dewey *How We Think* (D. C. Heath 1933)
2  *Mathematics in Primary Schools* (HMSO 1965)
3  *Primary Education* (HMSO 1959)
4  B. Inhelder and J. Piaget *The Growth of Logical Thinking from Childhood to Adolescence* (Routledge and Kegan Paul 1958)
5  G. Mialaret *The Psychology of the Use of Audio Visual Aids in Primary Education* (Harrap/UNESCO 1966)
6  J. Henry *Culture Against Men* (Tavistock Publications 1966)
7  R. G. Cave *Some Effects of Television Viewing on Children Living in a Rural Area* Diploma Thesis, Institute of Education, University of Bristol
8  J. D. Halloran *The Effects of Mass Communication* (Leicester University Press 1964)
9  F. W. Wertham *Seduction of the Innocent* (Rinehart, New York 1954)
10 *Report of the Committee on Broadcasting* the Pilkington Report (HMSO 1962)
11 Schools Council, *Working Paper No 2: Raising the School Leaving Age* (HMSO 1965)

# Chapter 7

# TOWARDS MUTUAL RESPECT

In the Plowden Report the following statement is made: 'What matters most are the attitudes of teachers to parents and parents to teachers—whether there is genuine mutual respect, whether parents understand what the schools are doing for their individual children and teachers realize how dependent they are on parental support.'

As we have seen there are some welcome indications that British teachers are, to an increasing extent, recognizing how dependent they are on this parental support. We have noted that it is mainly in the primary school that the most far reaching and revolutionary developments in home/school relationships are taking place. We have also examined some of the reasons why it is imperative that parents and teachers work together right from the start of compulsory schooling, or even earlier if possible. However, it would be over-optimistic to believe that the 'us' and 'them' mentality, which is still found in some sections of our society and which has such deep roots in our social system, will disappear overnight. In the hard core of educational priority areas most teachers are likely to be regarded as belonging to 'them'—the 'them' so brilliantly described by Professor Richard Hoggart:[1] 'the world of the bosses'—'the people who give you your dole, call you up, tell you to go to war, fine you,' 'get yer in the end,' 'are all twisters really,' 'never tell yer owt,' 'will do y' down if they can,' 'treat y' like muck.' Still, recent trends, strengthened as they are by official policy, do allow some grounds for at least a cautious optimism even so far as the most deprived neighbourhood is concerned. At the primary stage in education, especially towards the upper end of the junior school, it is often the children themselves who insist that parents and teachers should meet more frequently. In good progressive junior schools, the wide range and quality of the work produced by the children is such that many of them cajole and beg their parents, however reluctant they may be, to visit the school at every available opportunity. Unfortunately, this enthusiasm on the part of pupils for parental interest in their school work and the desire that their teachers and parents should meet often may disappear altogether at the secondary stage. Even at the primary stage there are some children who actively discourage their parents from visiting school, and there are of course parents who refuse to visit in spite of pleading from their youngsters. It is these parents, who either will not or cannot bring themselves to visit the school, who form the central problem in any attempt to improve home/school relationships in difficult areas.

Where parents, despite all efforts, will not come into the school some teachers have tried to improve cooperation by home visiting. One or two schools have in fact established posts of special responsibility for home/school relationships; in these schools home visits are part of the special teacher's normal duties, and provision is made for them in the time-table. Home visiting, especially in slum areas, can present a great many difficulties and such visits may pose problems even for trained social workers. In some neighbourhoods a visit from a teacher may be regarded with the same hostility or apprehension as a visit by a probation officer or policeman. Such visits are likely to endanger home/school relationships rather than cement them. On the other hand, in some homes the teacher may be made welcome when no one else from the world of 'them' would get a foot over the doorstep. A number of older teachers may find the idea of home visiting so foreign to them that it is unlikely they will ever take part in visits on any large scale. Younger teachers, however, influenced by the growing impact of sociology and sociological research on educational practice may in the future accept some home visiting as a normal part of their professional commitment. Certainly there are good grounds for suggesting that colleges and departments of education should include some discussion of home visits as part of the content of their education course.

Teachers, while they accept illiteracy as something one battles with in the school, sometimes forget that in the world outside the school there are many illiterate parents, some of them 'lapsed literates'. This poses a great many problems for the teacher wishing to make contact, as most of the traditional channels of communication between teacher and parent are closed. Commonsense dictates that if a letter has to be sent to a parent whom the teacher knows or suspects to be illiterate (or an immigrant who cannot read English) it should be as short and friendly as possible—parents will obviously not want a letter which has to be read to them to contain any criticism of themselves or their children. The mere problem of arranging to visit an illiterate home is difficult as arrangements may have to be made by word of mouth through the child. In general it is probably unwise to make unannounced visits except in emergencies, although in time a relationship may be established where a teacher can call at a child's home as a welcome friend and adviser. Parent/teacher friendships are likely to follow the same sort of pattern as any other relationships. They will thrive where they are to mutual advantage and wither where one or both parties find that they have neither anything to give nor anything to receive.

An experienced teacher can usually find some good excuse for visiting a home, however deprived, and if he is wise as well as experienced, certainly the first visit will take the form of a request for help on his part. Any visit to a disadvantaged home should, where possible, be a positive one, in the sense that it should be deliberately contrived to mitigate against the idea that anything which brings one of 'them' to the door must mean trouble. A school outing or trip can provide a good opportunity for a preliminary home visit and some teachers have been known to conduct 'surveys' of which the main, even if not published, object was to make personal contact with parents.

There are obvious dangers when people from contrasting

backgrounds first meet. Teachers by profession tend to be successful and competent talkers, while some of the parents they visit may rarely hold long conversations, and any attempt on their part to do so may be quite a strain. In some cases, therefore, initial visits should be short, perhaps lasting half an hour at the most. On the other hand, just as much tact needs to be exercised when the teacher finds himself in a home where the parents are happy to talk at great length, perhaps in a slanderous manner, about everybody and everything.

So much for visits. What about getting the average parent into the school? Many parents will quite happily come to formal functions such as prize days—although these are fast disappearing in progressive schools—or a swimming gala. Inevitably there is an artificial and forced atmosphere about these occasions. Teachers get little opportunity for useful conversation with parents and the parents get little idea of the real work that goes on in the school. Many heads, having found that such functions serve little purpose in improving home/school relationships, are experimenting with other methods. For example, Miss D. M. Smith, Headmistress of Fulbourn County Primary School, Cambridgeshire and Isle of Ely, has written the following note describing such an experiment:

In the past I have tried to encourage cooperation between home and school in various ways but, like other teachers, I have found that those I most want to meet never come near the school. I discussed this with my staff at a meeting last year at which we were arranging our usual 'Open Evening'. The staff said they dreaded this open evening which left them exhausted as queues of parents had waited to speak to them about their children. It was suggested that we should have an open fortnight for infants and the second week only for juniors, during which time the parents were invited to come at any time during school hours. We decided that nothing should be 'put on' for the parents but that they should see the school following the day-to-day routine. The parents were welcomed by me on arrival and told where they would find their children's classrooms. They went into the appropriate classroom, introduced themselves to the class teacher and stayed in the room for a while. We found the children were very pleased to see their parents and many parents who normally never came to school came because their children wanted them to come. Needless to say, we found oral class lessons were almost impossible during this fortnight as parents were free to come at any time but, as most teaching in the school is done by an individual approach, this was not too serious a problem. We followed this open fortnight by an 'At Home' one evening but we found that apart from being a pleasant party it served no real purpose. At the end of this experiment I asked for written comments from each member of staff. They were as follows:

'I had either one or both parents come during open fortnight, except for three. I think this was most successful. I think those parents who came along on the last evening were not sure why they were here. Most expected a more formal meeting for comments etc.'

'Only seven children did not have a parent come during the week and of these three came on the At Home expecting to see the children's work. This open fortnight disturbed the children tremendously but the parents were interested. Several said that they were sorry it was so late in the year and wondered if school could be opened permanently. I felt that the last evening was rather a waste of time since so few came and those who did did not know why.'

'Most successful but I think it would disturb the children less to have only two or three days open and not a whole week. The open evening, I found, was not needed.'

'All the children's parents came during the open week and only one on the late evening. I felt that both were not needed. Parents were very interested in the children's work and it proved to be beneficial spread over the week instead of chatting to many parents in one evening.'

'The open week was very successful in my opinion but

the evening was rather a waste of time as all but three of my parents had already seen me. I think that two or three days would be sufficient for the school to be open, thus cutting down the turmoil of having parents in.'

'Open fortnight I thought was very successful. Parents seemed to like the idea very much. I had only two fathers come to see me during the evening and I, therefore, feel that an evening follow-up is not needed. Of course, several parents in the class is naturally a disturbing factor and it excites the class.'

'I thought the idea of having two open weeks was very good and it helped the parents to appreciate our difficulties. The open evening was a little bewildering for some parents but it was nice to meet fathers as well. I must admit that the teaching was rather chaotic during the two open weeks.'

'I was impressed by the number of parents who came, especially those whom we seldom see on more formal occasions. The problems we have really hit them and this is having its effects. As no parents of children in my class came to the open evening my only comment is I could have done the ironing.'

Typical of parents' letters following this experiment is the following: 'Dear Miss Smith, I would like to say how much I appreciated the chance to see Martin with his class during normal class activities. I realize that having parents dropping in at any time of the day must have caused great inconvenience to staff and I feel they all deserve a special "thank you". I was also glad of the chance to have a talk with Martin's teacher. I think he was very lucky to have started his school career with her. He has been extremely happy ever since he started school and we are very pleased with his progress.'

Miss Smith's concluding comment was: 'We felt that the venture had been worthwhile but from the experience gained we hope to repeat it for shorter periods, or perhaps for afternoons only, to alleviate the disruptive element.'

This report and the teachers' comments are reproduced here

merely as an example of the way schools are making tentative experiments in an attempt to improve home/school relationships. Obviously in some cases it will take time and both parents and teachers will need to make a great many adjustments. However, it is only through such actual trial experiences that worthwhile methods will evolve.

Most head teachers see their work in home/school relationships as pioneering and some believe that such cooperation is way ahead of the wishes of most of their parents. For instance, in *The Times Educational Supplement* for 20th December 1968, a letter from a headmaster stated:

> The conclusions I draw are (a) that because I believe parent/teacher cooperation to be essential for the well-being of the school and try to enlarge this concept beyond the ordinary day routine I am well ahead of the demands or wishes of the great majority of parents; (b) that parental interest in education is too frequently limited to the attainments of their own child, but this is natural enough; (c) that parents are soon satiated with education talks, films etc, and that better attendance would probably be ensured if events of this nature were limited to once or twice a year; (d) that it is difficult to maintain teachers' enthusiasm in view of the lukewarm response of parents; (e) that the number of activists in the PTA is the same as in most other voluntary groups and that before we have any more suggestions/demands from ACE, 'Where' and the Home and School Council, they should examine the sociology of voluntary groups; (f) that for most parents the knowledge that they are free to attend school at almost any time, that the head teacher and staff are freely available, that the school is theirs, that a few functions are arranged each year, is sufficient. Probably the most important point is that they realize that the head teacher is human, subject to the usual weaknesses, does not act as a demi-god and accepts parents as equals. Once this has been achieved most of them are happy but this is not to say I think it enough.

Here then is another view which emphasizes the fact that

only by experiment will we reach a stage in our knowledge of the benefits of home/school cooperation where we know with any certainty what is 'enough'. As most of this book is being written in a deliberately optimistic—some will say utopian—vein, let us look at one or two views which underline the fact that there are people in the world of education who are more pessimistic. In a leader in *The Times Educational Supplement* for 15th November 1968, under the title 'Hands Across the Fence,' the following statement was made:

> Most parents are just not interested in education although Mr Edward Short is confident about an improvement in this sorry state of affairs. Let us hope that his optimism is justified but meanwhile it is evident that apart from the crusading minority, weary teachers and detached parents remain contentedly on each side of the educational fence. Parental non-involvement has a positive and a negative side. Priority families may have an undefined complex antagonism towards their children's mentors arising from the unfortunate authoritarian association with their own school days. A common middle-class attitude holds that teachers have a clearly defined job to do outside the limits of the home and that they should be left to get on with it uninterrupted. This view is heartily endorsed by many teachers dubious about the possible threat to discipline and professionalism constituted by the vision of uncontrolled parental interference with their work. Many have probably met and shrunk in horror from the keen, dynamic, graduate mum with firm ideas on education. Only a conviction of the educational validity of more home/school relationships will win over the unconverted teachers.

So much emphasis is placed in this country on voluntary participation that perhaps it is worth noting that parent/teacher cooperation is not always so free. For example, Joslyn Owen, Deputy Director of Education for Devon, writing in *Education* for 28th February 1969[2] had this to say about parent participation in the Federal Republic of Germany:

> With each year class within a school is associated a body

of parents—all the parents of all the children in the class. The teacher principally responsible for the class *has* to call a conference of parents four times each year. The agenda for each meeting has to include, as the first item, pedagogy. And the typical agenda concentrates on curriculum, on school organization and on social education. The normal pattern for each meeting is that of discussion, led by the teacher, a parent, or an outside speaker, followed by a new educational film; the Institute for Film in Learning and Education at Munich, jointly financed by *Länder* is said to be sufficiently active and well funded to ensure that very new films are always available. The teacher cannot skip one of these four annual class meetings; the right to demand them belongs to the parent. Two parents are elected as chairman and vice chairman by the class parents. The two chairmen of each class parents' group form a parent committee for the school. The chairman of the school parents' committee can call a conference on his own initiative, without reference to the head. And four school conferences *have* to be called each year. Teachers can be required, by the parents' committee, to attend and if a class parents' committee is dissatisfied with any aspect of teaching, the individual teacher can be called to account before the schools' parent committee. To balance this intense parental activity comparable regulations, *Konferenz Ordnungen,* apply to meetings of teachers. A staff conference has to be held once a month. The chairman and vice chairman of the schools' parent committee have to be present (i.e. the dates have to be fixed to suit them, not the teacher) and, also by regulation, two representatives of pupils must be present. These pupils are elected by the pupil-body.

Mr Owen, after describing some further aspects of parental involvement in the government of schools, goes on:

Doubtless, in view of their nervousness about the activities of something as innocent as the Home and School Council, some of our teacher associations would view the German system with abhorrence—perhaps an abhorrence equal to that which they would feel for the Soviet system of 'shame-boards' under which any one of eight different community bodies can call a teacher to public account. But to quote Gittins (out of context) 'the existence of other approaches at least raises the question of whether our own potentially autocratic system is necessarily the best.' We may raise our eyebrows at these foreign ways of doing things, but might they not at least give us some clues not only about the future of governors and managers but also about the full potential of parent involvement.

Certainly the suggestion that parents should be seen at least once a year does not sound so revolutionary when viewed in the context of the above. There is, of course, an important aspect of the growing concern with education on the part of parents which we have not yet considered. Education was a vital topic in the elections during the 1960s and it seems probable that it will continue to be so through the 1970s. The interest and involvement of parents in the educational process will inevitably be mobilized by the politicians, although it is to be hoped that in this country parents and teachers will accept voluntarily the type of cooperation that appears to necessitate legislation elsewhere. - Germany , USSR...

Mention in *The Times Educational Supplement* leader of the keen, dynamic graduate mum reminds one of the fact that if the primary school is the only truly comprehensive school in this country at present, then also it is the only school with a comprehensive range of parents. In practical terms primary teachers have to communicate in an effective manner over as wide a range as the illiterate parent to the university don. Such a wide range makes for obvious difficulty, not only in personal face-to-face contact but, as already mentioned, in letters and reports to the home. On the question of reports for parents Plowden says:

> Written reports in the past have often been a waste of time since they were so conventional that they conveyed nothing to parents. There is a genuine problem; parents

need to know how their children are getting on, yet some may fail to distinguish between effort and achievement or be wounded by the truth and discourage their children. Useful reports are difficult to write and take time. They are much more helpful if the teacher knows the parent for whom he is writing. On balance, we think it would be helpful if parents were given a written comment at least once a year.

The whole question of reporting to parents of primary school children is one about which there has been considerable and continuing controversy. Most people would agree that there is little point in making a detailed written report on children of infant school age. When we come to the junior school, however, there is some evidence to suggest, as indeed Plowden confirms, that the majority of parents would welcome some form of written report at least once a year. Obviously in the ideal parent/teacher situation where there are frequent face-to-face meetings between the parents and teacher, with the child's work available for discussion, there would be no need for any written report, except perhaps for record purposes. Under present circumstances, unfortunately, such an ideal state is rarely achieved except possibly in small rural schools, although in one or two of the larger urban schools, where there has been special emphasis on home/school relationships, this ideal may be approached even though it entails a great deal of planning and organization. In those cases where contact with some of the parents is infrequent or does not take place at all there would seem to be a need for the occasional written report.

The question that naturally follows is 'What form should such reports take?' Plowden has emphasized that 'written reports in the past have often been a waste of time since they were so conventional that they conveyed nothing to parents.' Perhaps Plowden is being overoptimistic in talking about conventional reports in the past tense. My own experience is that it is not unusual for even a progressive primary school to be making use of antiquated report forms. In some cases the blame for this can be laid at the door of the local education authority who may issue standard report forms, although this is happening less frequently now. There are many obvious difficulties in making a written report to parents on the progress made by their children—the central òne being that of finding a description which really conveys some meaning and accurate information. The old-fashioned report which consists of grades, exam and class positions is extremely misleading and may often cause a great deal of either unnecessary anxiety or foolish self-congratulation on the part of both parents and children. What, for example, does a mark of 5 out of 10 for Science mean?—or 83% for Art?—and yet both parents and child may attach such importance to these statements that they may have a damaging effect on the parents' opinion of the child and on the child's own self-picture. Traditional reports also usually assume that parents are only interested in the child's progress in the basic subjects when very often, in fact, they would also welcome information about behaviour and personal relationships. One of the more obvious factors working against the preparation of more detailed reports is that primary teachers may have little free time—parents do not always realize that teachers in primary schools, unlike their colleagues in the secondary schools, rarely, if ever, have non-teaching periods. Lawrence Green has suggested in *Parents and Teachers*[3] that schools might be closed occasionally for the express purpose of allowing teachers to prepare reports. I would not go all the way with this suggestion; where there are working mothers, for example, the closing of schools might cause ill rather than good feeling.

However it would be useful if extra secretarial help were available to teachers at certain times of the year. The description 'report' has in itself a forbidding ring to it. Several suggestions have been made for other terms such as 'development record' but so far none of these appears to have found general favour.

In many schools the old type of report has been replaced by a personal letter to each parent and some excellent examples of such letters are given in Education Survey No 5. Parents welcome praise and desperately need advice about how they can help when they are worried about their children's progress.

There is no point in the stereotyped 'could do better' unless some advice is given to parents on how they can help their children achieve this better performance. There is, of course, as we have noted, the problem of writing to parents who are themselves illiterate, and an even greater problem may arise when the parents are expected, as is happening in an increasing number of schools, to make comments—in other words, to write their own report for the teacher. Lawrence Green has proved in his own school that the great majority of parents will read reports and even in a poor area at least 60% of the parents will have something to write in reply.[4] These replies might take the form of a questionnaire, in which such questions as membership of clubs, libraries, hobbies and so on are asked. Some schools in the United States have been using this form of two-way report for many years and their experience has proved just how valuable this can be. Not only may the teacher learn much about the parents' view of the child but the reports may also clarify for the teacher what is of most value in the way of parent education. In addition such a questionnaire may enable the first contact to be made in establishing good parent/teacher relationships—the parent shows that he is worried about what his child reads at home or how he spends his leisure time, and the teacher may be able to make positive helpful suggestions.

As with reports, homework at the junior stage is another subject on which parents and teachers frequently appear to have diametrically opposed views. In the past, homework has been one of the traditional, although sometimes limited, links between home and school. As the junior school curriculum and the nature of cooperation between home and school is changing, so the traditional concept of homework is being re-examined. Plowden, basing their comments on the results of their parental survey, categorically state: 'Parents wish children to do school work at home' and then go on: 'Homework should be a matter for discussion and agreement between home and school and the school should give thought to the form of homework most suitable to children's varying circumstances.' There is a fair amount of reliable evidence to show that the selection examination at eleven-plus has, to a large extent, shaped the nature of homework in many schools.

Some teachers claim that homework for the probable grammar school entrants is necessary—if one school in an area sets it then the remainder must as well, so that their pupils will have a fair chance. In areas where the selection examination still applies, it is not uncommon for homework to be set only for those children who are likely to do well in such examinations, and often the pressure for homework for such children comes from the parents themselves. My own experience is that the majority of teachers in the junior school are against the old-fashioned homework where the child is expected to do so many 'examples' out of an arithmetic book. In the past this type of homework has all too often caused a great deal of emotional upset in the home. Children have shed countless tears and parents have felt considerable frustration because of such remarks as 'Miss doesn't like us to do it that way.' Even teachers may find it difficult to help their own children with work set by their school as so much emotional heat may be generated. Often a parent feels frustrated because the child does not seem to have a clear picture of what is expected of him; this leads to recrimination and emotional upset and cannot but harm home/school relationships as the parent may imagine that such upsets and misunderstandings are part of the ordinary day-to-day life of the school. Even where the fairly traditional type of homework is set, the school should attempt some guidance and make it very clear what is expected of the child and what part the parents are expected and encouraged to take. If the school, for example, insists that long division or subtraction should always be done in a certain manner this should be made clear to the parents. Special difficulties may present themselves when dealing with immigrant homes. Immigrants—especially those who come from a culture where much greater stress is placed on homework than in this country —often insist on homework for their children as 'they have so much to make up.' In contrast, some parents may be very critical of the basic skills type of homework on the grounds that children spend a fair proportion of their life in school and if the school cannot do its job without a great many extra hours, then something is wrong. So far as the junior school is concerned, I would find difficulty in countering this argument.

Instead of creating links, homework may in some cases positively impair relationships. Certainly homework which shows up inadequacies in the home, such as lack of books, cannot but fail to do this. Fortunately, there are signs that a new enlightened approach is being adopted. Less emphasis is being placed on mechanical tasks, although if practice in certain essentials such as basic number facts has occasionally to be undertaken, home may well be the right place for it.

In junior schools working along creative lines, there need be no sharp distinction between what is done in the school and what is done at home. As the selection examination is abolished it is a fairly safe prediction that more and more schools will abandon the old methods. Certainly it would be a pity if the old traditional homework lingered on after the eleven-plus examination had disappeared. On the other hand, there will always be a place for activities in the home—such as hearing a child read—to supplement work in the school. In schools which are working an integrated day, when each child keeps a record of the amount of time spent in different activities, there is no reason why home activities should not form part of the school's integrated approach. Homework in the progressive school is often concerned with the child's hobbies—a review of the book he has been reading or the continuation of some simple science experiment over the kitchen sink. Less emphasis is placed on written work. For instance, teachers may ask children to view a television programme and give a verbal report or criticism. As we have discussed, the whole field of leisure-time television viewing offers wonderful opportunities for parents to help develop in their children enquiring and discriminating minds. Where parents and children take part and enjoy home activities together the work of the school is strengthened and the false educational boundary between home and school becomes even more difficult to define.

References

1 R. Hoggart *The Uses of Literacy* (Chatto and Windus 1957, Penguin 1958)
2 J. Owen 'Can We Learn Anything from West Germany?' (*Education* 28th February 1969)
3 L. Green *Parents and Teachers* (Allen & Unwin 1968)
4 *Ibid*

Chapter 8

# LINKS AT THE SECONDARY STAGE

We have already discussed some of the problems associated
with transfer from home to school and from infant to junior
school and suggested that here is an area of mutual concern
where home/school cooperation is of the greatest importance.
At a later stage, when the transfer from junior to secondary
education occurs, problems are also raised which may be
considerably eased if parents and teachers work together. To
take one of the most obvious examples: it is not difficult to
imagine the possible misgivings of youngsters, perhaps trans-
ferring to a comprehensive school with a roll of over 1,000,
whose experience of school life to date had been in a one- or
two-teacher village school. The majority of boys and girls
appear to look forward to transfer to the secondary stage of
education and are stimulated and excited by the prospect of
going up to the 'big school'. For a few however it is a time of
strain, sometimes very severe strain, and in the past little
attention was paid to these unfortunate youngsters. Welcome
changes are rapidly coming about but it is still possible to find
primary and secondary schools which have little contact with
each other. In fact, there may even be some slight degree of
hostility between the head of the secondary school and the
heads of the contributory primary schools. Fortunately, such
situations are rare, especially in areas where associations of
parents and teachers span both age ranges, perhaps covering

the whole group of associated schools. Such associations have an important contribution to make in smoothing out some of the difficulties of transfer. In the past it was common to hear such complaints as 'I don't know what they do with them in the junior school' or, alternatively, 'I don't know what goes wrong with them when they go to secondary school.' If teachers voice such complaints today it can usually be regarded quite legitimately as a self-indictment. Secondary teachers who don't know what is happening in their contributory primary schools, or primary teachers who know little about the secondary school, very likely have no one but themselves to blame. Most teachers are only too happy to welcome colleagues concerned with other age ranges into their schools and see that everything possible is done to ensure that there is no sharp break, either in curriculum or method, when transfer takes place.

For some parents the meetings or interviews arranged at the primary school to explain the transfer procedure is their first contact with their children's teachers; if a good impression is made here it will obviously make it easier to continue good relationships into the secondary school. A number of interesting experiments are taking place in involving parents at this stage of education. For example, the Inner London Education Authority pamphlet *Home and School,* points out that transfer to the secondary school carries with it for both parents and children as many tensions as original entry to the infant school. It goes on to stress how important it is that parents fully understand the transfer procedure. They suggest that this can be ensured by parents' meetings or by letter, or by both, and 'This step must be followed by individual interviews at which the situation as it relates to each child is fully explained and parents are advised as to choice of secondary school.' The pamphlet goes on:

> In addition some junior heads make arrangements with their secondary colleagues for parents to visit secondary schools before the interview; others invite secondary heads to come and talk about their schools at parents' meetings. An interesting development in some junior schools is to ask parents to write their own report on their children for

transmission to the secondary school with the primary school's records. Parents have been responsive and the information offered about children's attitudes and interests has been frank and valuable.

In this book, I intend to omit any detailed discussion and make passing reference only to the reorganization of secondary education, a reorganization which is causing a great many headaches to teachers, administrators and of course to parents. So far as our subject here is concerned reorganization along comprehensive lines has, as in the case of the eleven-plus, had the effect of encouraging an active involvement on the part of those parents who think seriously about the educational provision which local authorities make for their children. It has also had the wholly welcome side effect of bringing those who administer education much closer into contact with the parents they serve.

It might be as well here to make some comments on the thorny subject of parental choice. The concept of parental choice derives from two provisions of the 1944 Education Act. The first provision is that part of the Act which makes it the duty of the parent of every child of compulsory school age to cause him or her to receive full-time education suitable to his or her age, ability and aptitude. The second provision is Section 76 of the Act, which reads as follows: 'In the exercise and performance of all powers and duties conferred and imposed on them by this Act the Minister and Local Education Authorities shall have regard to the general principle that so far as it is compatible with the provision of efficient instruction and training and the avoidance of unreasonable public expenditure pupils are to be educated in accordance with the wishes of their parents.' Obviously the proviso 'so far as it is compatible with the provision of efficient instruction and training and the avoidance of unreasonable public expenditure' has led to some practical limitations being placed on parental choice. These limitations are not always easy to explain to disappointed parents.

Much has been said and written about the reorganization of secondary education and I believe that concern about this subject has tended to lessen what I consider to be a far more important concern—the actual content of the secondary curriculum. However, no matter what form the organization of a secondary school may take, the need for good home/school relationships remains constant. Whether a 12-year-old boy is attending a secondary modern school, one of the new middle schools or a traditionally organized grammar school makes little difference to this aspect of his education. At the time of writing about 25% of our children are attending some type of comprehensive school and an increasing number are attending schools which form part of a two-tier system; in this system parental choice is a major factor in determining whether the children go on to an academic course. Thus primary and secondary teachers have a heavy responsibility for parent education and guidance.

In general, home/school links are much more difficult to forge at secondary than at primary level. One of the more obvious reasons for this was touched upon by Miss Alice Bacon, Minister of State, when she was addressing an international conference on parent education, held at Leeds in April 1969. Miss Bacon, after announcing that the Department of Education and Science were working on a guide for secondary schools on parent/teacher relationships, went on to say that the size of secondary schools and their distance from pupils' homes made links more difficult to establish. She also emphasized that special efforts are needed to see that a reduction in the rate of progress by the child is not accompanied by a diminution of parental interest, each accelerating the other. Certainly, there is some concern in the minds of both parents and teachers that the introduction of large comprehensive schools will be detrimental to good home/school relationships just because of the sheer size of these schools, although a recent piece of research[1] has shown that this fear is somewhat exaggerated; in fact out of 331 comprehensive schools surveyed, half had some form of parent teacher association. However, close links between parents and teachers are obviously easier to forge in small areas of homogeneous population, such as is usual in a primary school catchment area, than in the wider and often much more socially mixed area of a large secondary modern or compre-

Parents, teachers and pupils attend a fair sponsored by the PTA.

Parents and pupils attend a careers conference. Good home/school cooperation can do much to ease the pupils' transition from school to work.

HENRY GRANT

hensive school. Miss Bacon's anxiety about the possibility of a reduction in the rate of progress by the child being accompanied by a diminution of parental interest is of the greatest importance. Experience shows that unless special efforts are made, the gap in communication and understanding between teachers and parents widens at the secondary stage to an extent which a great many parents find impossible to bridge. Whatever views may be held within the profession itself, there is ample evidence that a good many parents regard secondary teachers as a very different kind of being from primary teachers. If questioned parents often say they feel more uncomfortable, less sure of their ground and uncertain of their welcome when they show an interest in the progress of their child at this stage in education.

Some of the London comprehensive schools have found that the employment of teacher/counsellors has helped to improve home/school relationships. In the Schools Council publication *Counselling in Schools*, Working Paper No 15,[2] there is a description of the work of a home liaison officer appointed to the staff of a secondary modern girls' school in a socially deprived area. When the head first took up her appointment 11 years ago she found that most of the parents were apathetic and a few were even antagonistic. Absenteeism was very bad, and the only parents to visit the school were usually angry and belligerent ones. It was decided that the staff must 'make friends' with the parents and that this object could best be achieved not by the visits of a social worker with only a slight connection with the school but by a member of staff—'someone who was so completely a member of the school community that when she visited the homes she would be in a position to speak from the teacher's point of view from firsthand experience, thus creating the much needed bridge from school to home'. Accordingly, a home liaison officer was appointed and a pattern was established which included visits to the homes of new entrants at the beginning of the year, followed by visits to the homes of second, third and fourth year pupils. The headmistress goes on:

The work that the liaison officer does in the homes is as varied as are the parents! In the homes of really interested parents she will have to discuss the school syllabus in detail, our philosophy of education, future prospects for the child, homework and so on. In another home, she will have to separate quarrelling parents and appeal to them to think of the children. In yet another home she will try and arouse the interest of parents who have always been too shy and embarrassed to dare show any! And, of course, she still teaches for two days a week. It is significant that she has made no bad relationships with parents and is always welcomed and her visit is becoming a status symbol. 'Miss, you 'aven't been to our 'ouse yet.'

I consider this appointment to be most important and useful to the school, especially as to the children and parents the liaison officer is a teacher who has 'come to see us'. She has the unanimous support of the staff who wonder how we ever ran a school before she came. There has been a more relaxed atmosphere in the school because of fewer tensions and improved attitudes on the part of the children. There has been an exceedingly small number of children before the courts, and the belligerent parent is a rarity. The academic achievements of the children have increased because of the backing of the home, and their ability to do homework and the encouragement they receive.

The above arrangement is very much in line with the recommendations made in paragraph 204 of the Newsom Report:

The schools cannot do the job alone, and parents cannot delegate their responsibility for guiding their children. Many situations would be helped simply by the schools knowing more of the home circumstances and the parents knowing more of what goes on in school. All existing links, such as parent teacher associations, open days, invitations to school functions and concerts, conferences, regular school reports and, most of all, informal conversations between teachers and parents, are extremely valuable. But there is a percentage of homes—and in some districts, a majority—which such arrangements do not touch. In dealing with these problems, the schools and the parents need special help. There may be a strong case for having additional members of staff who have special responsibilities for home visiting, and who act as liaison officers with all the other medical, welfare and child care services in the district. This also implies a need for teachers whose training has included some realistic sociological studies.

The practical results of special appointments such as those described have shown that it is simply not true that working-class parents do not welcome contact with the school; they also emphasize that it is the school which should first extend the hand of friendship. Unfortunately, there are still secondary schools where the whole idea of trying to draw the parents, especially of deprived children, into the education process is viewed with a great deal of suspicion. One occasionally meets a secondary head, described by Sir Cyril Norwood as 'the autocrat of autocrats,' who appears to have an ingrained mistrust of parents, especially the parent whose own background has left him or her in ignorance of the aims and objectives of modern secondary education. For much of this century many people have had the opinion—an opinion probably having its roots in the nineteenth century—that it was the business of the school to 'eliminate the influence of parents on the life chances of the young'.[3] The educators' job was to pull the boy or girl, especially the bright boy or girl, out of his neighbourhood and family mores and attitudes and set him firmly on the path to middle-class success. The Newsom Report concept of the teacher acting as 'a liaison between school and neighbourhood' is totally foreign to those people who think along these lines, especially those who serve or have served in grammar schools, where the tradition so often appears to have been to cut the child off from his roots. Jackson and Marsden have dealt fully with this in their book *Education and the Working-Class*.[4]

Professor Mays has stated in a recent book:[5]

Perhaps all one can say is that many heads are opposed to too close a tie up between home and school, few are in favour, and a fair number are either neutral or refuse to come down on one side or the other. Indeed, the very fact that so much emphasis has been placed on *specific* kinds of school-home liaison in recent years may in the event have helped only to stiffen resistance to all such suggestions and produced a reaction of hostility from some head teachers who may well believe that the criticisms and suggestions which have lately been offered to them are uninformed and even misguided.

In spite, then, of all that has been written in Newsom and Plowden, in a variety of journals and individual books, it seems likely that the teaching profession is far from being committed to a policy of all-out liaison with its local community and that many heads and assistants wish to preserve a degree of social distance between themselves and the parents of their pupils.

No doubt some of the material in this book will be described as 'uninformed and even misguided' but it is important to stress once again that we are in a state of rapid transition. This is difficult to prove statistically as no really up-to-date survey of teachers' and parents' opinions on cooperation exists. There are, of course, those who believe that parent/teacher cooperation at the secondary stage is something that will come about only very slowly. My own view is not so pessimistic. For the majority of schools, cooperation along the lines shown by the best examples may indeed lie largely in the future, but some changes are taking place now. One factor that may influence teachers is the realization that parents are also voters and that increasing involvement in education on the part of parents is the best guarantee of professional status and a bigger slice of the national cake for education.

While the verbal, involved, middle-class parent will make sure his child gets the best possible deal from the existing system, experience suggests that a great many working-class parents of young school leavers are just as anxious about the education their children are receiving but are both nervous about approaching the school and ignorant of the part they are expected to play. Some rather dated research findings are available on this subject. As part of the preparation for the raising of the school leaving age the Government Social Survey carried out an enquiry into *Young School Leavers*.[6] The survey was based on the assumption that schools are 'likely to be most successful with those pupils who are supported by their parents and whose interests, motivation and sense of relevance are captured by the work they do'. The findings were based on interviews with 1,489 teachers in secondary schools; 4,546 parents; 4,618 thirteen- to sixteen-year-olds; and 3,421 young people, aged nineteen to twenty years, who had left school. The report states:

> In the national survey among parents who had children in maintained primary schools, carried out for the Plowden Committee, 8% had had no real talk with the head or with their child's class teacher. Among parents in non-manual occupations the figure was 5% and in manual occupations 9%. At the time of that survey the children whose parents were interviewed were almost equally divided between the top junior, bottom junior and top infant classes. In the present enquiry, in which the children were in the third, fourth or fifth years of their secondary schools, 37% of the parents had had no real talks at all with the head or any of the child's class teachers at the sampled schools.... Among the 15-year-old leavers, 38% of the parents in non-manual occupations had not had talks with the school staff, in skilled manual occupations the proportion was 46% and in semi and unskilled occupations it rose to 54%.

In the North and Midlands rather fewer parents of 15-year-old leavers had talks with school staffs than in the South; in secondary modern schools 41% had not had such talks compared with 24% in grammar schools.

When the teachers' opinions were sought it was discovered that in general heads were more inclined than teachers to think that the schools did have the positive support of the parents of 15-year-old leavers, and that the great majority held the view that it was all important for school staffs to take positive steps to encourage parents to visit the school regularly. Only 11% thought there was no point in trying to persuade apathetic parents to come. It was found that over half the parents of 15-year-old leavers felt they were interfering if they went to the school uninvited. This general reluctance of parents to 'interfere' was highlighted by the success of the Advisory Centre for Education's 'education shop' which showed that the parents of secondary school age boys and girls welcomed advice when it was made easily available.[7] In *Young School Leavers* it is categorically stated that 'half the parents of 15-year-old leavers were anxious to be told more about how their child was getting on at school and a third felt that teachers should to a greater extent consult them about their child.' Secondary teachers need to take positive steps to contact parents, especially bearing in mind the attitude of working-class parents that the only time one should visit the school is when something is wrong.[8] It is of course unwise to assume that silence always signifies approval. Even if it is only a small minority of parents who express dissatisfaction this may merely mean that they don't miss what they have never had. Teachers need to do whatever they can to maintain a balance with regard to over-involvement on the part of the unduly anxious parent and non-involvement on the part of the type of parent we have just discussed. As Douglas has shown[9] the middle-class 'have retained almost intact their historic advantage over the working-class' in the schools. Criticism from a section of the population, which to date has been happy to delegate all responsibility, would be a small price for the schools to pay for the gains that would inevitably follow from improved contact over the whole of the social and economic range from which they draw their pupils.

References

1 M. Cox (ed) *One School for All* (NFER 1969)
2 Schools Council *Working Paper No 15: Counselling in Schools* (HMSO 1967)
3 F. Musgrove *The Family, Education and Society* (Routledge and Kegan Paul 1966)
4 B. Jackson and D. Marsden *Education and the Working Class* (Routledge and Kegan Paul 1962, Penguin 1966)
5 B. Allen (ed) *Headship in the 1970s* (Basil Blackwell 1968)
6 Schools Council *Enquiry One: Young School Leavers* (HMSO 1968)
7 *The Education Shop* (Advisory Centre for Education, Cambridge 1965)
8 E. Midwinter 'The Parents' Case' *Times Educational Supplement* 25th July 1969
9 J. W. B. Douglas *All Our Future* (Peter Davies 1968)

# Chapter 9

# A RELEVANT CURRICULUM

A possible difficulty, although one which can be changed into an advantage in strengthening cooperation and communication between parents and teachers at the secondary stage, is that in many secondary modern schools, and to a lesser extent in some grammar schools, the content of the curriculum is changing rapidly. As we have noted, many teachers themselves find it difficult to adjust to the demands made on them for a fresh approach—so it is hardly surprising that a great many parents, even those who try to keep themselves well informed, feel confused.

One of the most exacting and yet rewarding tasks facing educationists at this time is the devising of a relevant and meaningful curriculum for secondary boys and girls of average and below average academic ability. The proposed raising of the school leaving age means that the new fifth forms will include 60% more of the age group than was voluntarily staying on at the time the government initially announced that new legislation would be introduced. Devising a relevant curriculum for the full five years of secondary education for all is an undertaking which calls for an entirely new conception of the importance of a partnership between parents and teachers, a partnership which should also include the pupils themselves. The suggestion that pupils—students is perhaps a better word—should be concerned in the planning of at least part of their own education is no longer the revolutionary or impracticable suggestion it would have been considered a few years ago. Parents and teachers will know that one of the more significant differences between the primary child and the secondary student is that the older boy or girl, quite justifiably, is beginning to assess critically the education he is being offered and may ask 'What real relevance has this subject or activity for me?'

As the end of their schooldays approaches students have to make choices with important practical consequences. It is at this stage that one can really begin to judge the success of the educational approach which has been adopted in the preceding years. Anxiety about future employment prospects may lead young people and their parents to place an unwise emphasis on vocational subjects, and a vital part of parent education in the secondary school is to clarify the relevance and importance of such aspects of a modern secondary approach as education for personal responsibility and the growth of thinking and communication skills. The fact that an increasing number of young people are staying on at school voluntarily, even when not examination candidates, is an indication that many schools are providing for the less academically able boys and girls an education which makes sense to both students and parents.

A few secondary schools have experimented with bringing in the parents to help with the actual work of the school; this is especially true where the Newsom recommendations for an extended day are being put into practice. For a variety of reasons, not least of which is the difficulty of making extra payments to teachers, the extended day in secondary schools is slow to start in some areas. As more schools do adopt the extended day, it will likely prove to be a part of school life where parents can play an active role. In discussing the extension of the school day, the Newsom Report says: 'The situation might be further helped if the schools, as a matter of policy as well as a way of increasing their own staff resources, deliberately sought the assistance in some extra-curricular activities of local experts and enthusiastic members of adult clubs, some of whom might well be found among the parents.' This paragraph was written mainly with physical activities in mind but there seems no reason why the idea should not be extended to cover intellectual and social activities. There are other ways in which parents can help with the extended day. For example, a rota of parents could help to solve the problem of returning youngsters to their homes—this is especially important in rural areas—or help with refreshments.

So far as the normal school curriculum is concerned, perhaps it is mainly in the practical subjects that auxiliary parental help will make its main contribution. To date only a few rather hesitant and tentative experiments have been undertaken. One can see that in domestic science or home economics, many parents might have a useful specialist contribution to make, just as in art and crafts, woodwork and metalwork, a parent with specialist skills might give valuable help. Language teaching is another possible subject, as is music. Some schools already make use of parents for individual instruction in musical instruments and a number have formed orchestras composed of parents, teachers and children. Parents have also traditionally helped with physical education activities, especially those that take place at the weekend or in the evening. Where schools are experimenting with such subjects as home maintenance, electrical engineering, motorcycle maintenance, boat building and so on, assistance by parents has already proved invaluable.

Obviously such liaison and cooperation is much easier to establish in a community or neighbourhood school. Several recent official reports, including Newsom and Plowden, have mentioned the contribution that the Cambridgeshire Village Colleges have made towards the concept of the community school, and if some of the suggestions made in this book seem over-optimistic it is perhaps because I have had the opportunity of being closely involved, for the past ten years, with the Village Colleges and their contributory primary schools. The distinctive feature of the village colleges, the first of which was opened in 1930, is that they comprise a combination of secondary school and community centre, providing for the intellectual, social and recreational life for a rural, and now in some part a semi-rural, area. They were conceived as a way of providing the countryside with cultural opportunities in no way inferior to those provided in the towns. Much of the basic philosophy is applicable to both urban and rural life and the programme of activities differs from one college to another, according to the individual needs of the district and the tastes of the students. Courses are provided for those who wish to take examinations such as GCE; liberal studies programmes are arranged in consultation with the University of Cambridge Department of Extra-Mural Studies, the WEA and similar adult education organizations; and high standards are obtained in a variety of crafts such as pottery, sculpture, carving, wood and metalwork. Adults and young people come together for a variety of activities and the specially provided village college youth centres make it possible for young people to enjoy a pleasant social environment, where they can work out their relationships with one another and where there is unobtrusive adult fellowship and understanding when needed.

The common-room and lecture room of each College are used by the parents and by other adults during the day as well as during the evening. The common-room is used by the Parish Council, the Infant Welfare Clinic and the Over-Sixties Club. Births and deaths are registered there as well. Self government is the essence of the adult activities of village colleges. Students' councils, which are representative bodies of all students, undertake the arrangements for numerous social functions, visits to other educational establishments, weekend courses, and the provision of amenities which cannot be provided by the local education authority. In such an environment there is nothing odd about adults, including parents, being part of the school during the day.

Many parents express genuine surprise that most young people now actively enjoy subjects which, in their own school-days, meant long hours of dull, repetitive work. For example, modern mathematics is now regarded primarily as the discovery of relationships and although there are certain facts which must be learnt and practised, the subject now includes a great deal of experiment and enquiry. A wide variety of apparatus is used, and average secondary students tackle subjects that at one time would have been thought too difficult even for the high flyers in the grammar school. In progressive schools most of the mathematical activity centres on a room or rooms designated as a mathematics laboratory. In such schools all manner of equipment is used—surveying instruments, desk calculators, simple computers, models of switching circuits and so on. Enthusiasts for the new approach point out that even with non-examination pupils, the aim of mathematics teaching is not only skill in computation, but also the development of judgment, imagination and adaptability. One secondary school has even purchased and runs a small trawler as a going business concern. The opportunities in this latter case for such mathematical topics as navigation, marketing methods and accountancy can easily be imagined, as can the wide variety of other educational experiences such a project offers. Progressive work in mathematics has involved parents in the making of a film on the mathematics of the village and the building of an astronomical observatory.

In secondary schools experimenting with progressive methods, the emphasis in the teaching of science is similar to the modern primary approach. Students are given every possible opportunity to discover and experience things for themselves. Teachers in favour of this approach make the work as realistic as possible, following the Newsom recommendation that 'To our boys and girls "realistic" means belonging to the real world, that is the world of men and women, not of school children.' Once again there are many opportunities here for parental participation. Mention of the 'real world' brings us to another new development in our secondary schools—a development given considerable emphasis in the Newsom Report: 'The field in which it is most important that boys and girls should learn to exercise a commonsense judgment quickened by imaginative insight is that of personal relations.' There have always been enlightened teachers in secondary schools who have recognized the importance of education for personal responsibility, and in the past few years there has been a marked increase in those who would agree with the view that 'the young people in our schools should be encouraged to develop judgment by discussing problems of adolescence within the school setting.'[1] A variety of techniques are used, including unscripted drama, tape recordings, film, real life situations (perhaps taken from newspapers), and discussions are encouraged on such topics as relationships with friends and relatives, boy and girl friendships, race prejudice and so on. The aim is always to find 'starting points' along the lines suggested in paragraph 321 of the Newsom Report:

> To set a class to study a clearly defined problem in human conduct and human relations into which boys and girls can project themselves and work out the various implications of different courses of action—this is realistic teaching. It is also imaginative teaching. Indeed very often the only way to be realistic is to use the imagination as an aid to responsible living, thus developing conscience from the stage of taboo to the level of insight.

An increasing number of young people stay on at school after the compulsory leaving age, and this trend is likely to continue. Obviously, the fifth and sixth forms will, and do, contain many boys and girls who are involved in a strong emotional relationship with a member of the opposite sex. The physical and emotional aspects of love and sex will be tentatively and, in some cases, extensively explored, and both parents and teachers will need to come to terms with the knowledge that this is so. That change is taking place in this area of adolescent behaviour is certain, but the extent of the change is difficult for parents and teachers to assess. The most detailed piece of research on this subject is that undertaken by the team led by Michael Schofield, published in 1965 under the title *The Sexual Behaviour of Young People*.[2] The findings revealed that by the age of sixteen, 14% of the boys and 5% of the girls in the sample had experienced sexual intercourse, usually with somebody who was older and more experienced. Schofield states:

> Half the boys and 14% of the girls did not receive any sex education at school. In all types of state schools, including grammar schools, as often as not there was no sex education for the boys. The lack of sex education was exactly where it was most needed; it was the working-class boys who were the least likely to learn about sex from their parents and were least likely to receive sex education at school.

Certainly there are many schools where such facts of modern life as earlier physical maturation, the increase in unsupervised association between the sexes and the current trend towards very early courtship and marriage are almost completely ignored as important factors affecting their pupils. In such schools, sex education, where it exists at all, is mainly concerned with descriptions of secondary sex characteristics or solemn warnings about the risk of pregnancy and the dangers of contracting venereal disease. Even in progressive schools it is only within recent years that the emotional aspect of relationships between the sexes has been seen as a suitable subject for discussion. A great deal of re-thinking about sex education appears to be necessary. Although it is obviously important to educate for family life in the sense that marriage and parenthood are of great concern to the majority of young people, it is unrealistic to carry out such a programme without taking into account the experiences students may be having at the moment. Some education authorities tackle the problem in a thorough manner. For example, in 1964 the City of Birmingham Education Committee set up a Working Party to study and report on the place of sex education in the schools.[3] A survey was made and the replies to the questionnaire showed that, although almost every school taking part in the survey agreed that information about venereal disease should be given to the older pupils, about one-fifth of the schools were not tackling this subject at all. Most schools felt it was necessary to discuss and give guidance to older pupils on matters such as promiscuity and adultery, and there was clear evidence that 'secondary schools as a whole believe that more information should be given to older pupils on family planning, birth control and contraception.' However, about 50% of the schools were not anxious to embark upon the principles of birth control and contraception in any great detail. The final report produced by the Working Party is a most enlightened and heartening document and one might hope that its use will not be confined to schools in the Birmingham area.

The whole subject of sex education in schools is an area fraught with the danger of misunderstanding between the school and the parent, but it is also an area presenting great opportunities for parent/teacher cooperation. Neither side can claim a monopoly of knowledge or experience, and parents and teachers working together can come to much more useful conclusions than if they worked alone. As the Scottish Education Department's publication *Raising the School Leaving Age*,[4] points out: 'Indeed the importance of ensuring that young people acquire a sound moral code by which to regulate their lives is of such vital importance that the support of the home and the community must be enlisted. The school can provide the meeting place.'

Finally, let us look briefly at examinations—a subject that causes concern and emotional involvement on the part of parents and teachers. I have already commented on the fact that the introduction of the eleven-plus examination, especially when fee-paying was abolished in grammar schools, made for a much greater involvement on the part of parents. For a variety of reasons, some of which we have already discussed, the growth of examinations in the secondary modern school did not at first have the same effect. It is the case however that by the 1950s more and more secondary modern schools began to enter their pupils for examinations other than the General Certificate of Education, mainly because of the growing demand from both parents and employers for some paper qualifications for students attending non-selective secondary schools. In some areas, once again mainly in response to the demands of employers and parents, schools and local education authorities established local leaving certificates.

A great many parents are still confused about the pattern of examinations at the secondary stage, and many secondary teachers make use of this uncertainty in a final attempt to bring parents into partnership. Obviously, where there is a choice of subject or examination offered, it is as well to do everything possible to explain what is happening. Many parents are confused about the fact that John or Mary can take science or history, but not both, and wonder why other subjects are adopted or dropped. Especially confusing is the fact that some schools offer GCE others CSE and some a mixture of both. It seems probable that with the raising of the school leaving age an increasing number of children will have a large part of their secondary education shaped by the demands of examinations. A joint report of the Standing Conference on University Entrance and the Schools Council, published in December 1969, is likely to have far reaching effects on sixth form studies if its proposals are adopted. The report recommends two new examinations: 'Qualifying' and 'Further'. The qualifying examination (Q level) would be taken after one year in the sixth form in a maximum of five subjects so grouped as to ensure a wide range of studies. Five passes at Q level would become the basic entry requirement for all forms of higher education. Those students who wished to go to a university would take a maximum of three subjects in the further examination (F level) at the end of their second year in the sixth form. So far as the secondary modern school is concerned the first flush of anti-examination feeling, which followed the 1944 Education Act, was gradually replaced by an increasing acceptance of examinations; teachers and parents discovered that the eleven-plus selection procedure was by no means infallible in selecting those children who might do well in examinations at the age of 16. The GCE was introduced in the summer of 1950 and was primarily designed for pupils in grammar schools, but increasing numbers of secondary modern pupils were entered for this examination. A complicating factor, so far as parents were concerned, was that in some areas secondary modern pupils who wished to take the GCE examination were encouraged to transfer to technical colleges, or late transfers to grammar schools were arranged. However there was growing discontent with the fact that for many boys and girls there was no opportunity to study for GCE in their own schools. In 1953 half the secondary modern schools in the country had no fifth forms. By the early 1950s more and more boys and girls were entered for examinations other than GCE—for example, those set by such bodies as the Royal Society of Arts and the Union of Lancashire and Cheshire Institutes.

By 1958 the number of examinations for pupils in non-selective schools appeared to be getting out of hand. A special committee of the Secondary Schools Examination Council was set up to study examinations other than GCE, and this committee recommended that a new examination, to be known as the

Certificate of Secondary Education, should be instituted. Examinations for this new certificate were held for the first time in 1965.

Many parents find it puzzling that some heads believe that it is in the best interests of pupils, even those of fairly low academic ability, to enter for the CSE examination. Examination Bulletin No 1 points out some of the possible disadvantages of examinations for all ability ranges in the secondary modern school.[5] It states:

> The Certificate of Secondary Education makes no claim that examinations can assess the many intangibles that go to make a successful education. Parents and users of the Certificate must be positively encouraged to seek other additional evidence of the qualities and human capacities of school leavers. Nor must the schools forget those not taking courses leading to public examinations: the non-academic or Newsom pupils.

Although the CSE examination is gaining recognition by an increasing number of employers and professional bodies, many parents still regard it as inferior to the GCE, and there may be obvious conflict in the home when a child is trying hard but his parents disparage the objectives towards which he is working.

It would be a great pity if the only conversation some parents have with their child's teachers at the secondary stage is on the question of whether to leave school or to stay for a further year. The answer to this sort of question is often decided by the quality of the home/school relationship in earlier years. The teacher whose first request for an interview with parents comes when the child is fifteen is some years too late. It is distressing to learn, for example, that according to a survey published by the Merseyside Child Poverty Action Group, only 29% of Merseyside families in poverty know that educational maintenance grants are available to enable children to stay on at school after the age of 15. As Douglas' research has shown, the influence of the home is greatest at two periods; 'first during the pre-school years and second at the end of the compulsory school period when many pupils leave, including a number of very able boys and girls'.[6] This is a tragic waste of talent and ability and makes nonsense of our claim that all children have equal educational opportunities.

References

1 *Half Our Future* the Newsom Report (HMSO 1963)
2 M. Schofield *The Sexual Behaviour of Young People* (Longmans 1965)
3 City of Birmingham Education Committee *Sex Education in Schools* (Report of the Working Party on Sex Education 1965)
4 Scottish Education Department *Raising the School Leaving Age: Suggestions for Courses* (HMSO 1966)
5 *Examinations Bulletin No. 1: Some Suggestions for Teachers and Examiners* (HMSO 1963)
6 J. W. B. Douglas *All Our Future* (Peter Davies 1968)

# Chapter 10

# FROM SCHOOL TO WORK

When the student is ready to leave school or move on to higher education, good home/school cooperation faces one of its main tasks. It is sometimes claimed that most working-class parents show little real interest in the efforts made by careers teachers and agencies, such as the Careers Advisory Office, to help their children find suitable employment. Figures can be quoted to support this claim; for instance, only about 50% of parents take advantage of the opportunity to attend the interview that their children have with careers advisory officers. This however is in many ways as much an indictment of the relationship built up between the home and the school in the years preceding the interview, as it is a reflection of apathy or indifference on the part of the parents. In many cases the main responsibility for failure to build up a relationship lies with the school. Admittedly, the most sincere and persistent efforts may fail, but the school should at least attempt all that is possible to establish a relationship which will be to the advantage of the children for whom it exists.

Many working-class parents do want more information about careers for their children. The Schools Council enquiry on *Young School Leavers* gives statistics:

It has already been shown in Chapter 2 of this section that most parents and children considered that teaching pupils about the different types of jobs and careers available and preparing them for their first experience of working life were very important functions of the school. Parents in general would themselves also have valued more information about jobs and careers and advice about their children's capabilities so that they could be of greater help to them in deciding on suitable work. Of parents of 15-year-old leavers, 71% wanted more help for their child in actually finding a job, 64% would themselves have liked to know more about different types of jobs available and 62% wanted more guidance on their child's abilities.

Once again the main emphasis will be placed on the provision made for the children of the lower income and less educated groups in our society, as it is in this section of our school population that there is the most pressing need for improved home/school relationships. Even the parents of those children who have managed to find a place in the grammar schools often find themselves in difficulties. As Jackson and Marsden point out in *Education and the Working-Class*:[1]

There was bewilderment of almost every conceivable and utterly basic kind. Parents were unable to communicate their needs to teachers, and teachers steadily mistook the level and nature of inquiry. Such parents were not wanting to know whether Anne could beat another girl in history, or whether she grasped the second law of thermodynamics. This information was welcome, and often useful—but it hung over a void. They wanted to know what physics *was* and what kinds of jobs it opened for a girl; they wanted to know whether you could do anything with a history qualification except teach more history. They wanted to know the difference between a training college and a university, in nature, quality, time, cost. They wanted to know if their son could even think of becoming a doctor after taking languages in the sixth form. Or what it meant in terms of future choice when their daughter had to abandon chemistry or Latin at 13; or whether there was any difference between the universities at Bangor and Oxford; or any difference between going into the Civil Service at 18 or taking a degree first. A hundred and one problems of this kind troubled their relationships with school and child.

Since Jackson and Marsden's book was written, Douglas' research[2] has more than emphasized that although in theory the road to suitable careers and higher education is open to all, in practice the career choice and the level of aspiration may be seriously depressed for no other reason than lack of information on the part of the parents. Even where pupils' academic ability and intelligence are similar, parents in the different social classes have very different ambitions for their children. For example, Douglas has shown that 'the low expectations of the manual working-class parents may reflect the real difficulties that many talented pupils have in attempting to enter the professions when they lack skilled advice and encouragement from their parents and schools.' The last part of this sentence is most disquieting. The fact that boys and girls may receive little skilled advice and encouragement from their parents may be no fault of the parents—but the fact that even our brightest boys and girls may receive very little useful advice on choice of career or higher education from the schools is a problem which must be faced and remedied as soon as possible.

In the autumn of 1967 there were about 370,000 students following advanced courses in Great Britain—54% in the universities, 29% in colleges of education and 17% in the technical and other colleges. Once the school leaving age is raised and there is an increasing number of pupils staying on at school long enough to gain minimum qualifications for higher education, it is inevitable that this number will rise rapidly. Increasing numbers of parents will be confused by the choice of higher education offered and will need to know more about the opportunities provided by colleges of technology, colleges of commerce, technical colleges and the new polytechnics. Schools will need to explain to parents the exact place of such institutions as colleges of art and colleges of agriculture, together with the bewildering university and college of education system. There is of course another side to the problem. In the book *Headship in the 1970s* Cyril Poster points out:

149

Though there is this wide acceptance of the general benefit of extended education, there is a good deal less understanding of what it means, what it demands of the youngsters, what support parents can give to the idea of work at this level even if they do not understand the content, and above all what it can lead to. Parents of potential candidates for higher education places have had to be convinced that their children were worthy of the chance; the safe apprenticeship or good office job represented the peak of their ambition. Other parents, on the other hand, encourage children in wild dreams: a career as a vet for a girl who 'just loves animals' (but has little academic ability and does not like science) is our annual nightmare. Careers guidance in the normal sense is a non-starter in conditions like this. It pre-supposes a reasonable equation between ambition and ability.

Important as is adequate guidance for higher education candidates and their parents, the problem of career choice for the young school leaver is every bit as pressing. There is little point in improving secondary education for boys and girls of average and below average ability if insufficient attention is paid to them when they move on to the world of work. For too long in this country the whole question of vocationally biased education in the secondary modern school has been debated on an emotional rather than a rational level. It is not difficult to understand some of the historical and ethical reasons for the objection to vocational education on the part of many teachers, especially those who are themselves first generation grammar school. Certainly the argument that the job of the school is to give as wide an education as possible and not just to provide more effective units for industry is still advanced very strongly today. Charity James, in her book *Young Lives at Stake*,[3] says:

> By setting pre-vocational studies in the context of Special Interest we acknowledged the validity of any interests that genuinely involve the young; there is no need for any aspect of life to be eschewed by a school except the practice of vice or crime. At the same time, we are taking a necessary

step of liberating school from the special responsibility it was engaged in for preparation for jobs. With the setting up of the Industrial Training Boards, which are charged with this function and can fulfil it effectively, the national requirement that society makes of schools has been clearly de-limited. We now know, both from the findings of the Crowther Report and those concerned with the Industrial Training Act, as well as from conversation with good employers, that for young school leavers the most important qualification is a sound general education.

One of the difficulties in the past has been that two sets of sub-cultural values have combined to trap young people in vocational courses, sometimes of a narrowly conceived kind; these are the belief of working-class boys (and to a lesser extent girls) that adult status consists of going to work and earning a living and the middle-class dedication to notions of personal vocation and of the virtue of work for its own sake. Often the courses proposed have been of little value since for some higher levels of skills the machines available have been far too old-fashioned and for many young school leavers the whole notion of pre-vocational studies is inappropriate anyway as their work does not recognize such skills.

Many educationists appear to have a very narrow view of vocational education and, as is so often the case in educational controversy, much of the disagreement appears to stem from an inadequate definition of the terms used. The Newsom Report appealed for 'more outward-looking adult-life orientated programmes for those less bright children who are determined to start their working lives at the earliest opportunity' and recommended: 'The school programme in the final year ought to be deliberately out-going—an initiation into the adult world of work and leisure.' In the sense I would wish to use the term, education for personal responsibility along the lines discussed in the last chapter is very much part of this concept of vocational education.

This brings us to one of the central problems facing those who are concerned about the relationship of home and school

and stress the value of cooperation in helping prepare youngsters for the transition from school to work—a change in their
lives which has been compared by one writer to an adult
emigrating to another country. Evidence shows that the
majority of parents feel that the schools' main objective should
be to help achieve good job prospects. Teaching staff, on the
other hand, are increasingly concerned with the wider aims
of education. If good relationships have been established and
the school has tackled parent education right from the early
years, this apparent dichotomy of interest should not prove
too great a gap to span. As I have discussed in detail elsewhere[4]
the progressive educator's aim of education for living and the
parents' desire for an education that has direct relevance to
vocational choice can be combined. Indeed one of the aims of
introducing the vocational element into secondary schools is
to improve the value of secondary education by cashing in on
an obvious source of motivation. It is important of course to
avoid disappointment insofar as the schools should ensure that
they give neither the parents nor the pupils false hopes of the
benefits to be received from vocational education, either in
its narrow sense or in the wide sense that I am discussing here.
However most young people do not make unrealistic choices.
In fact, as was stressed above, there is a large group of young
men and women who, though potentially capable of entering
one of the professions, choose manual work. They are unable
to see themselves following a different way of life from their
parents and friends. If the nation is to avoid such wastage in
the future—a wastage we can ill afford—vocational guidance
must start with the parents and begin in the early days of
secondary schooling. The main aim at this stage is to change the
traditional outlook, which in the past has been moulded all
too firmly by family and neighbourhood values.

Special attention needs to be paid to vocational guidance
for girls. Most girls obviously look forward to marriage as their
main career but it is important for the high flyers to plan their
careers from a long-term point of view. They may well marry
early but after they have raised their families, many will want
to either resume or begin a career.

Working-class parents have a strong influence on their

child's career choice. Although the choice may in many cases appear to be made by the boy or girl, in fact the parents usually still choose the first job for their child; they need help and guidance in this important decision. Teachers may take a long view in contrast to parents who press their child to go into an occupation which may no longer even exist in a few years' time. Fortunately however most parents are no longer mainly interested in short-term financial gains and are anxious to do the best they can for their children. The schools and careers advisers have the task of ensuring that the young school leavers and their parents are aware of the ever widening choices available. Such vague statements as 'I hope he'll have a trade' or 'I'd like her to work in a clean job' need to be clarified, not dismissed as irrelevant or stereotyped ambitions. So far we have stressed the information and help that the teacher or careers advisory officer can give to the parents. There is, of course, the other side of the coin. As in education for living courses, parents may be able to give a great deal of help in explaining the facts about the world of work to the boys and girls in the school. In this field they may really be the experts. In the old days many young people learnt about the work their fathers and uncles did by visiting the place of employment, perhaps to take their fathers' dinners at mid-day. Such first-hand acquaintance is rarely possible now. Some parents would no doubt be willing to play their part in talking to the young about their jobs, and the young are realists enough to take notice of what those actually doing the job say about it. Parents can also help in the preparation and display of reference materials, perhaps bringing actual materials from their place of work. Parents might also keep careers teachers in touch with vacancies in their own firms and help teachers in their choice of speakers. In some secondary schools one finds the most bizarre occupations and professions represented by speakers, although the people the pupils would most like to hear might be the local garage mechanic, shop assistant or hairdresser. As the Newsom Report emphasized: 'A major problem is how to ensure that the teachers themselves apart from having the right contacts and the necessary sources of information really understand the work situation as their pupils will meet it.' Here indeed is an area where parents can make a most valuable contribution.

An increasing number of educationists believe it is important to give their pupils real experience in the world of work while still at school. Visits are arranged to provide boys and girls in the last year at school with experience of the working world, which will help ease the transition from school to work. A minority of parents may not be in favour of work experience, preferring the school to stick to its traditional role—once again here is a need for parental education. We have already mentioned the increasing employment of counsellors in British schools. It may be that in the future some of the men and women who, as parents, give voluntary help in such work may find there is a place for them in the profession. Counselling is likely to attract many who would not be interested in normal teaching, and this may be all to the good as the desirable qualities are neither primarily nor necessarily academic.

Much of the argument in this book has tended to the belief that many of the tasks that are either not done at all or are done inadequately by teachers, because of lack of time or specialist knowledge, may be and should be performed by the parents. Education is preparation for the real world; the use of men and women from the outside world in counselling about career prospects or in helping solve pupils' personal problems emphasizes that the sharp division drawn between the professional educator and the parent should not exist in the schools of the future. Home/school cooperation is not something that may happen—it *is* happening. We would be wise to welcome and encourage this partnership for change.

References

1  B. Jackson and D. Marsden *Education and the Working Class* (Routledge and Kegan Paul 1962, Pelican 1966)
2  J. W. B. Douglas *All Our Future* (Peter Davies 1968)
3  C. James *Young Lives at Stake* (Collins 1968)
4  R. G. Cave *All Their Future* (Penguin 1968)

# VOLUNTARY BODIES

The Nursery Schools Association of Great Britain and Ireland, 89 Stamford Street, London SE 1

National Society of Children's Nurseries, 45 Russell Square, London WC 1

National Association of Pre-School Playgroups, 149 Fleet Street, London EC 4

The Pre-School Playgroups Association, 87a Borough High Street, London SE 1

The Save the Children Fund, 29 Queen Anne's Gate, London SW 1

Council for Children's Welfare, 183–189 Finchley Road, London NW 3

National Federation of Parent Teacher Associations, Honorary Joint Secretaries:
Mrs M. L. Swinson, 10 Stoke Newington Church Street, London N 16
Miss P. Girling, 5 Elm Terrace, Tividale Hall Estate, Dudley, Worcestershire

Advisory Centre for Education, 32 Trumpington Street, Cambridge

Confederation of Associations for the Advancement of State Education, Honorary Secretary:
Mrs D. Lamb, 9 Addison Road, Great Ayton, Middlesbrough, Yorkshire

The Home and School Council, Field Officer and Director:
Mr R. A. Finch, Derwent College, University of York, Heslington, York

# Index

adventure playgrounds 61
Advisory Centre for Education 16,
31, 134, 157
Association for the Advancement of
State Education 16

Bar Hill Pre-School Playgroup 37–40
*Black Papers* 69–70, 80–2, 87
book exhibitions 88–90
Bowlby, Dr John 27–8
Boyle, Sir Edward 19
British and Foreign Schools Society
11

Cambridgeshire Village Colleges
138–9
Central Advisory Council 17–8
Comprehensive Schools' Committee
16
compulsory education, growth of 9–
11
compulsory school attendance 14
Confederation of Associations for the
Advancement of State Education
157
contributions of parents to schools
60–4
    making and repairing toys 60–1

digging ponds 61
caring for animals 62
light construction 62
helping physically handicapped
children 62
repairing books 63
making and showing films 63
providing transportation 63
typing and duplicating 63
Council for Children's Welfare 157
counselling 129, 154
critical periods in growth 25
Cross Commission 12
Crowther Report 18, 151
CSE 145
curriculum reform 66–70

developmental approach 24–30
Dewey, John 17, 48–50, 82

Ede, Chuter 13
Education Act of 1870 13–4, 46
Education Act of 1902 12, 13
Education Act of 1918 15, 33
Education Act of 1921 33
Education Act of 1936 15
Education Act of 1944 12–3, 15, 17,
32, 33, 66, 127, 144